Early Reading

A Paperback Original
First published 1990 by
Poolbeg Press Ltd.,
Knocksedan House,
Swords, Co. Dublin, Ireland.

© 1990 Máire Mullarney

ISBN 1 85371 097 0

Cover design by Pomphrey Associates
Typeset by Typeform Ltd.
Printed by The Guernsey Press Ltd.,
Vale, Guernsey, Channel Islands.

Early Reading
A Guide for Parents
Máire Mullarney

POOLBEG

Contents

The Debate about Reading

Introduction

This book has two beginnings; one for some, one for others. Some readers will take it for granted that reading is pleasant as well as useful and that children who pick up the skill early are lucky. They may have been told—no-one ever remembers—that they themselves were reading at three or four. They are simply interested in sharing, and perhaps profiting from, the experience of someone who has had unusually good opportunities for exploring ways of helping her own children.

These are the "some" who will begin with the first chapter.

Others more or less identify "reading instruction" with school. They believe it is wrong to force or push small children. Well, so do I. I suggest they go at once to the second half of the book, the section called "The Debate About Reading."

Well, perhaps not quite at once. I had better say a little about the experience on which I base my suggestions.

First of all, my husband and I read. We read at meals, we read in bed; I read in the bath, he doesn't. I too often read gardening books instead of going out and digging. He reads about Napoleon instead of cutting the grass. We are aware that an addiction to reading has drawbacks, but it brought us together—we found we had been reading the same books.

We married, at least in part, in order to continue reading together. We were somewhat interrupted by the arrival of eleven children. But while the first was only a few months old her father brought home a book about the beginnings of the Montessori movement. We were both much impressed. I mean, both parents were impressed, but baby Barbara took very readily to our home-made versions of Montessori's "didactic apparatus"; I'm sure it sounds better in Italian.

But the "didactic apparatus" is only a part of the Montessori Method. More important is the recognition that children are people who get satisfaction from work and who need to have suitable work made available. If they have this, whether they find it for themselves or are given it, they will often lose themselves in concentration for quite long periods. It is also important that they choose their own work, so if parents are offering special materials they should offer a choice, with the third choice of crawling or trotting away.

The child must always be free to take it or leave it alone.

And "work" covers a wide field. Pouring water carefully, drinking without spilling, helping to clean up the high-chair after meals; putting on socks or coat, later on tying shoelaces; helping to polish windows, use a dustpan; the maxim that goes with that is:

Never do anything for a child that she can do for herself.

In our household drawing and painting and gardening were constant activities, music just in the background. In other homes music may take first place. We were lucky enough not to have television when the children were small.

But in this book I mean to stress reading and the lead-up to reading, so I shall summarise our experience.

When Barbara was going on for three, the age when Montessori had introduced her children to letters, I tried to interest her in cut-out sandpaper letters. They were only about one and a half inches high and I found later that Montessori's had been twice that size; whatever the reason, perhaps because she was so busy about other things, and had already been tracing similar letters in a book of writing patterns, she was not interested. But her little brother, fifteen months younger, was very keen to know what was going on. Later, I came across several different accounts that told of babies under two showing spontaneous interest in letters, as Alasdar did. So I told him the sounds to associate with them (not "letter names") and around his second birthday he found out how letters make words and from then on there was no stopping him; he read his first book in a single day when he was three. The steps in between are the theme of the first part of this book.

It is probably relevant that Sean and I were, in effect, only children and that we lived almost in isolation, so that we had no idea of what was expected from children—at that time received opinion was that "reading readiness" was not be expected before the age of six. We were pleased about Alasdar's reading but not astonished; it seemed only reasonable to offer much the same experience, slightly modified, to the next two girls, Tinu and Janet.

Doubt began only when I bought the teacher's book that went with the series of *Beacon Readers*. This series had been very helpful indeed. It contained good traditional stories, often including repetition, like the one about the old woman whose pig wouldn't get over the stile. I could remember how I had enjoyed reciting that when I was three. The special feature of the *Beacon* series was that the vocabularies of the stories were carefully matched with phonic lists of words of graduated difficulty at the back of each book. Teachers were recommended to go through some lists each day before beginning reading and warned at intervals, "Do not go beyond this page until list XV is familiar."

This had worked very comfortably for our children. Because they knew any new tricky words before they read a story they could get through it straight away, and moved very quickly from reading aloud to reading for themselves. We did not repeat a story unless the child was specially fond of it.

Now, when I learnt that the designers of this trusted series were telling me that I had gone about things in the wrong way I naturally believed them. I bought the two "introductory" books of whose existence I had been unaware and used them with the next two children. The first one, *Kitty and Rover,* began with sentences: "Kitty sees the ball." When the child would repeat that on sight, from a flash card and from the book, you offered two flash cards, one saying "Kitty sees," the other "the ball."

This system went on, page after page, leading, I think, to a total "sight vocabulary" of about thirty words. I supposed I was doing the right thing, but I noticed more and more that the two children had trouble distinguishing lower-case "b" and "d" and some other letters. They never came to me insisting that I listen to them reading, as their siblings had done. Instead, we had to turn back the pages of *Kitty and Rover* over and over again to remind the reader of a word in the context in which it had been seen before. Indeed, this was so tiresome that I tried teaching the second of this pair the sounds of letters, but for lower case letters, not capitals. This did not help very much: when we reached the reading books with phonics and stories they were not nearly so competent as their elders had been. It might have been temperament, but I have no reason to think so.

So, for the next three, two boys and a girl, I reverted to the approach I used earlier, which I now call "Early Three–Dimensional Phonic Capitals" and everything went as smoothly as anyone could wish. For example, when congregations at mass in Ireland were first encouraged to speak in response to the priest saying mass this youngest girl was five; I remember listening to her beside me, reading the Creed without hesitation. She was very good, too, at catching the rhythm when reading verse she had never seen before.

5

But then I read an article by Glenn Doman. He told the world that children are much smarter than we suppose. They like to read early. He described babies of little over a year "reading" flash cards and going on to books made up from these words, eventually progressing to letters and their sounds.

I had two good reasons to be interested. Of the last two boys, the elder, when over two, had still not spoken at all, so the lead-up to phonic capitals wasn't possible. At the same time I saw a notice in church asking for help with a brain-damaged child. I found that quite near me was a family whose eldest boy was brain damaged. They had brought him to the institute in Philadelphia set up by Glenn Doman. The work-plan they were given was very intensive indeed and required many volunteer helpers to give passive movement exercises and to cajole the child into crawling for an hour or more a day. I agreed to go up every morning to help with the exercise. It didn't take very long; I usually brought my own two with me. I found that Alan's mother was doing wonders with teaching him to read according, more or less, to Doman's method, which is described in his book, *Teach Your Baby to Read*.

One day the elder of my last two was sitting in the garden. He was two and a quarter, still hadn't said anything much beyond "Mama" and "Dada". I heard him talking to himself. He was going through night prayers: "God bless Mama an' Dada an' Barbara an' Alasdar an' Tinu an' Janet . . ." right down the family. I hurried into the house, took four wide strips of white card and a red marker, and wrote MAMA, JANET, EOIN (his

6

own name) AIDAN. I sat down and waited. When he wandered in I took him on my knee and showed him two of the cards, using the "three steps" (to be explained quite soon.) I asked him, "Show me MAMA? Show me AIDAN?" He got them right, and *said* them. He noticed that I had two more cards. He wanted to see these, and he got these right as well. You could say, well, it was a fifty/fifty chance. But the next morning, when he came down to breakfast, he saw one corner of a card projecting from a shelf above his head, made it clear that he wanted the cards. He took one from me, said "Mama–no, Janet" and then named the other three correctly.

After that, it is not surprising that I became enthusiastic for this version of the "whole word approach." I offered Oliver, fifteen months, his favourite word, which was BIRDY. Because Eoin's talking had been delayed (we found later that he was partially deaf) I could play word games with both of them together. We had a good deal of fun with slugs and goldfish and birds eating worms and ourselves running and jumping and swimming.

The trouble began when each had a "sight vocabulary" of about 130 words, some in lower case, most in capitals. They began to confuse one word with another and this annoyed them. I had by this time taught them the sounds attached to letters, but they had become accustomed to words signalling their meaning at a glance and they resented suggestions that they go back to the beginning of the word and puzzle it out a bit at a time.

The result was that the youngest, who could,

apparently, remember pages at a time, and appear to "read" them if he had heard them once, but couldn't work out words for himself, went on strike when he was three. He would say that he would read to me if I read to him first, but then he'd be "too tired". You can hardly tell a three-year old that he's cheating.

(But is it any wonder children have difficulties; I have just looked at that last sentence; the first "read" is pronounced "reed", the second, "red.")

The older chap relied on guessing. Both were reading books in quantity by the time they were seven, but their progress had been erratic and their spelling compared very badly with that of their early 3-D siblings.

Our own eleven were not the end of my experience. The eldest grandchild, about eight years younger than his youngest uncle, lived with us for six months; between two and two-and-a-half, a very interesting stage. His mother, our second daughter, had taught him the letter sounds; I was not only able to help with the next bit, but to catch him on tape reading some of his cards, with enjoyment that can still be heard.

To bring the story up-to-date, I have spent most of last year looking after my youngest daughter's baby, all day, while she was at work, until he was fifteen months old, and seeing him most days since then; he is now about nineteen months. His approach to "structured material" like geometrical insets or nesting cups is not the same as that of the generation before him. His youngest uncle put a whole set of insets in their correct places, unprompted, when he was about fifteen months old. Until very recently, such things did not interest this last little chap. His concentration was differently directed. First, it was important to be standing; then, great concern about walking and climbing stairs. As soon as he could crawl upstairs, it was essential to walk up, clinging to the banisters. He was early taught to slide down backwards, on his blue denim tummy. That is not dignified; he has to walk down like other people, frontwards, taking, if possible, one step at a time. For quite a while another person would walk anxiously down in front, facing him, but now we trust him. And just within the last month he has decided that he wants to build up towers of nesting cups, put at least some of the insets in place, make cogwheels turn and have particular pages of his favourite books read to him over and over again.

I bring him into the story because he's different. My exploration of different methods of reading instruction made a rather good experiment precisely because the children taking part were well matched socially and biologically—same parents, same background, apart from having different places in the family, while their instructor did not think she was running an experiment—each time she changed she thought she was doing the best thing.

Not that our eleven were all the same; they have taken a variety of paths, but all had a good deal of experience in common and all of those who were led by means of Early 3-D to read independently at an earlier age, were distinctly better at spelling, which is one half of literacy whether we like it or not, and tended to do better in exams. "Tended", because the two youngest, the ones who tried the Doman way, have coped rather well with examinations.

9

Useful as this experience has been, I acknowledge that it is limited. I widened it theoretically by joining the UK Reading Association and then the International Reading Association, getting their journals for, it seems, eight years, even going to conferences. When most of the children were launched it seemed to me that the years of learning at home, before they went to school had been more influential than the years of school. I wrote a book, *Anything School Can Do, You Can Do Better*, which went into paperback and is now out of print. It told about the reading experience, but I deliberately avoided emphasis on this and saved all my arguments for a final chapter, which contained a good deal of the material in the second section of this book. I was perhaps too successful: there were many favourable reviews, but all spread themselves on atmosphere, art, de-schooling and life in a large family. Not one review mentioned reading and ninety per cent of the letters that flowed on for several years were looking for information about the mathematical material which had, alas, been discontinued. This is why I have decided in this book to focus on reading and let art look after itself.

Feedback was very encouraging, but more relevant to the present task is the fact that, soon after *Anything* . . . was published, I found myself free to "go to college"—to do a graduate diploma in theoretical linguistics in Trinity College, Dublin, a one-year course.

I enjoyed this greatly. My principal purpose was to try to find out the value of Esperanto, which I had learnt a year or so earlier, but I found that

"Reading Acquisition" was one component of the course. I felt that I had some hard-won expert knowledge in this field, so I decided to do two shorter final papers instead of one more substantial one, giving half my attention to each subject.

Both essays turned out to be longer than I intended. In the course of researching them I found that Esperanto was even more remarkable than I had supposed; I also found that there was a satisfactory supply of up-to-the-minute research on reading in the library of Institúid Teangeolaíochta Éireann, the linguistics institute. The more I read, the more I found that my views were becoming fashionable. About these views, which in fact are rather old-fashioned, and about what others have found through more formal research, I write in the second section of this book.

To summarise, then: the eleven children in our family learnt according to four different approaches, which between them cover almost everything that is or was recommended, plus our own Early 3D Phonic Capitals. Six used that method and learnt without effort. On average they were reading independently at four—one at three, another at five. The eldest child had been offered something much the same but apparently too late; the fact that her younger brother took to it so readily probably made it less attractive.

One child met whole sentences in lower case, another, letters and words in lower case, both using the same introductory reading book. Later, by comparison of workbooks, it could be seen that these two lagged behind their siblings by two years. More important, they didn't enjoy the early stages of reading nearly as much. The last two children, who were given whole words in capitals, did have plenty of fun at first, but did not progress smoothly and missed the side-benefit of picking up spelling without effort.

It is said that children will learn to read if they have stories read to them. That's a common factor to all the approaches we used, including, of course, the one described in this book. We both read to the children for hours and years, or years of hours, and enjoyed it. Some young people are able to drive properly the first time they sit in the driver's seat, because they have been watching carefully but most find that some methodical instruction is helpful.

We carefully avoided teaching them the names of letters; these merely cause confusion. This is discussed in the second section. Alphabetical order they met in exercises in their workbooks when they were five or six; a junior dictionary should do as well.

This book is about something more than helping young children to read. I see it also as helping parents to realise how competent they are, encouraging them to rely on themselves, and to explore with delight our children's unrecognised abilities.

1

What Baby Can Do

Unless this happens to be the very first book concerned with babies that you have read, much of what I am going to say at this stage will seem familiar. Familiar or not, you may wonder why a baby who cannot even sit up should be mentioned in a book about reading. Have patience and I think you will see how one thing leads to another.

You will have been told before that baby, when she is awake, should have something to look at; babies who cry a great deal may be quiet if they are held and encouraged to focus on something bright and shiny; a single pearl or a button on a background of black velvet has been recommended.

Babies feel safe when they are in touch with another human being; we know that mothers in many traditional cultures keep their babies with them in a sling of one kind or another. If it is not possible to hold your baby all the time she is awake she will like to be propped up where she can see what is going on; strapped into a reclining seat she will be safe. Here I warn from experience that it is impossible to overestimate a baby's ability to roll off a bed, table or chair; I learnt to change nappies either on my knee or on a waterproof cushion on the floor.

When carrying baby around, sing, whether you can or not. I cannot sing, but babies seem pleased by my rumble of "Little Boy Blue, come blow your horn" or "Rock-a-bye baby, in the tree-top."

Don't forget to support the clever little head until the fragile neck is strong enough to hold it. If baby spends some time on his tummy on a rug he will strengthen his neck muscles while trying to look around.

Then he will be able for more vigourous exercise, held standing on your knee and bouncing up and down to verse. A favourite of ours is "Up the airy mountain, down the rushy glen . . ." The thing to remember here is to let him do most of the work; if you put too much energy into it you might, as it were, jostle his brain.

It is best to ration radio and television pretty tightly. If there is always noise going on which means nothing to a baby she finds it more difficult to pay attention to something that has meaning. If you provide music on tape you will be able to play the pieces to which she responds as often as she likes. You can listen together, perhaps dancing, but keep it clear and gentle, Haydn or Handel, Mozart. Vivaldi, Telemann are easy to find, often in bargain tapes. Contemporary music doesn't seem baby-friendly.

Once you have a baby sitting up using his hands, give him small things to feel, things of wood, metal, fur, stone; heavy and light; bells and celery, gloves and necklaces. In the bath, not only corks that float, but filled plastic bottles that don't, egg-cups that sometimes do and sometimes not.

You do not have to be encouraged to talk to

baby about these things. Instinct will direct you to say, clearly, in a special voice, "Box, box," and "Stone, feel, stone," to talk about water and about being wet and dry and pouring and splashing.

The "Three Steps" which I mentioned in the Introduction are just an extension of this natural behaviour, but they have a peculiar value.

You just naturally say "Shoe" when you are about to put one on baby's foot; you have to plan to say, before that "Sock; sock." Then, *if he's interested* "Shoe; shoe. Give me sock? Give me shoe?"

It may not produce any response; he may give you a shoe when you have asked for a sock. Accept it; do not correct him. If anyone has made a mistake, you have, by asking him something he's not ready for. Not that you have done the least harm; on the contrary, you have learnt that not every thing you say is getting through. People sometimes think it amusing to ask a small child, beginning to speak, "What's that? What's that?" without having even told her. Whether she remains silent or guesses wrongly, her confidence is not going to be boosted.

So, these first two steps, which allow you to find out how much your baby is able to absorb at the moment, are very useful. You can use them with spoon and fork, Teddy and ball, saucepan and lid, any pair of convenient objects in which your pupil is interested. If she didn't get the right answer, wait a while before trying again. If she did, you can spend a few minutes a day trying new pairs until the pattern of information and question is familiar, and she knows that she's able to do something you appreciate.

How do you express appreciation? Families have different styles. I took part not long ago in a three-day seminar given by an Israeli professor whose concern was just this; how mothers "mediate" to their children all sorts of different facets of life. She argued that it was essential that mothers call the young child's attention to beauty in flowers, to order in things, to helpfulness in people, and so on. I shall quote a little:

Most known theories of child or personality development relate to the accumulation of success experiences, i.e., to the sum of successes or failures. This criterion relates not only to the direct exposure to success, but to its "interpretation" by a human agent as to the place of these experiences in relation to other behaviours that led to success, including the mental processes which preceded it . . . Through mediated feelings of competence, a child may not only learn that he or she has been successful, but also what components of their behaviour produced the desired outcome.

Professor Klein held that children who miss the sort of interchange with an adult where the child comes to recognise that the adult is showing— "mediating"—some action that has meaning, which requires the child to respond appropriately, is likely to grow up with "blurred undifferentiated perceptions and responses."

In other words, the child is likely to grow up dull.

Now, Professor Klein said that in her culture approval will be shown quite warmly and loudly;

16

she felt that northern Europeans play it very cool. I think we can tell from the baby's response whether she knows that she's done well; some of us show it one way, some another. If we go overboard about quite small things there isn't much in reserve for surprising victories.

But show it we must; in this country we are far more inclined to be negative; to correct with energy, to take achievement for granted. I am not thinking only of babies but of children and teenagers. Parents should talk about this together; people who have not been praised themselves seem to find it amazingly difficult to tell a ten or twelve year old that they've done really well and that father is delighted.

I daresay that seems to be looking very far ahead when we have just been looking at a baby strapped into a reclining seat, or sitting on a parent's knee, having five little piggies wiggled into a sock. But it's the patterns laid down in these few months—the first 18 months, according to the Harvard Pre-School Project (1972)—that last a life-time, and parents are building their style of parenting at the same time.

Anytime now you can offer one of those small books with pictures of objects that baby might recognise. Remember, even as you offer it, that in cultures without paper and books, like the pygmies of Central Africa, even very intelligent adults do not make the connection between line and colour and the solid objects they represent. You can put baby's favourite bunch of keys on the page beside a picture of a bunch of keys and, at first, get no response. It will come. Libraries can be very helpful in providing variety but she must have some books of her own, to which she can return over and over again, once she has made that connection.

By this time baby has been crawling, perhaps walking, climbing stairs, throwing balls (plastic, with holes, from sports shops, don't go too far, don't do damage); could be painting or sticking sticklebricks or trying to sweep crumbs into a dustpan. As I have said, I do not intend to discuss any of these enjoyments ; the purpose of this book is to describe a sequence which may be expected to lead into reading, but part of that sequence is awareness, is being *free to take it or leave it alone*.

And the complement of that freedom is being allowed to experience concentration. It may be experienced in carefully carrying a trowelful of earth from one side of the garden to the other, it may be in chasing one slice of carrot with her spoon; it is valuable, even irreplaceable and should not be interrupted. The maxim that may remind you of this is Professor Jerome Bruner's criterion for good child care: *The style of care that increases a child's capacity to manage its own attention.*

The other maxim I have quoted, *The child must always be free to take it or leave it alone,* comes from Professor J. McVicar Hunt. He advocated early learning, early cognitive development, as the only way to break the cycle of poverty and deprivation. He had found that babies and children need to have, and like to have, something on hand that is a challenge, that stretches their growing abilities, but had found it a problem to know how to avoid offering things that were too difficult, that would just provoke discouragement.

The solution he found in Montessori's system of showing children just how something should be used and then leaving the choice up to them, which means having two or three options available.

One choice that is available in almost any household is a set of pots/saucepans with lids. I have just read that microwaves are so popular in the US that "stovetop" cooking is going out of fashion. Well, I think that will be a backward step for humankind, if it ever happens, not least because of the absence from the environment of round lids and the various hollow objects on which they fit. All you have to do is put a sitting-up, slightly crawling baby on the kitchen floor, surrounded by lidded pots. Pots are best to begin with for two reasons, one because baby sees them in use, probably senses that they are part of the real world with which he is so anxious to be involved. The other reason is simply that they are round and have substantial handles so they are easy to manipulate and fit more readily than any other shape. They are also of different sizes, so that a small lid will fall down inside the too-large container, and the worker will have to try again. Of course a lid that is too large will sit in position; much reasoning power has to be developed before a child works out that, if he ends up with a non-matching saucepan and lid, there must have been a mistake further back.

Watching that power develop is one of the most rewarding parts of parenting. To help it develop you have to guard against interruption.

The price of it is having to tidy up and put away your whole collection when baby decides that he has finished his task.

You may not entirely enjoy moving out of the kitchen and handing over boxes and ornaments that have lids for taking on and off.

If you have around you objects so valuable that you would be angry with baby if he broke one you had better lock them away for a couple of years. I mean *lock*. Once a baby begins to move, he begins to explore. You must arrange a really safe place for cleaning materials and garden stuff, so put your ornaments there. It's not the breakage I am concerned about, but the risk of anger. There is no place at all for anger between adult and child. You will shout with alarm, perhaps weep with exhaustion, but it is we who have landed our babies in a world not designed for them and we have no right to be angry while they try to find their way.

Do not suppose that I mean children should be free to fiddle with everything that is not locked up. Since I have been minding a mobile grandson I realise how many more things there are to switch on and off than there were even twenty years ago: tape-recorders, television, dishwashers, automatic washing machines, word-processors. I have always tried to avoid the blunt, "no!" It's a very easy word to say, without deciding on the relative importance of the intended activity, and it's just as easy to learn, so that a child with only a few words may enjoy saying "no!" to every suggestion. I am quite certain that my charge must not turn the dials on the washing -machine. If he looks as if he wants to I explain this firmly. He doesn't understand the words, but he understands the tone; fortunately, the room that it is in has a bolt high up on the outside of the door. When he wants to open the door of the fridge, I say, "Not the fridge," and direct him towards another nearby narrow door, tell him that is his door. But when he insists on pressing the "Stop/Eject." button on the tape-recorder I just say, "Well. Now you've done it. No more music."

But even the modern home is not entirely electronic. It's lucky if you have some containers made out of wood or straw or papier-mâché that have lids and drawers that can be examined without causing anxiety. Help baby to feel the smooth surface of a heavy glass paper-weight, the ridges on a shell, show him how to blow out a candle and to blow away dandelion "clocks." Enjoy yourselves, and meanwhile plan to offer materials specially designed for fitting and matching. These we will discuss in the next chapter.

2

Structured Material

Do not postpone reading this until your baby has reached the stage discussed at the end of the first chapter. By that time there will a good chance that she is ready to profit from planned materials, but if she is to profit, you have to have them ready: nesting cups or boxes graded in size, pegs that will hold one, two, three, four reels (spools). More directly related to later reading is a set of geometrical insets, on these lines.

Now, there are at least three ways of providing these, some better than others. The best, I'm pretty sure, is to make them yourself out of plywood or get a more gifted friend to do so. One alternative is to buy something similar, called a form board, which has a number of quite small shaped pieces, each with a knob or handle, which can be lifted out and replaced. The other possibility is to buy a set made from plastic.

The advantage of the form board is that each piece, being wooden, has satisfactory thickness and when it's put in place it stays there. The disadvantage is that the layer with different shaped holes in it is fastened to a backing, so the apertures cannot be used as templates—that is, you cannot put them down on paper and trace through them.

The disadvantage of the plastic set, which has about a dozen different shapes, is that it is thin and has a tendency to slide. Even when an inset has been placed correctly an unskilled hand is very likely to push part of it under the edge of the frame. Also, the set most readily available lacks proper knobs or handles; there is a small central projection into which we have found it possible to glue the plastic markers from an old game of Chinese Chequers.

But the reason for putting the frame on paper and tracing around the inside edge is to develop "hand and eye control" and prepare for writing. We found this most valuable and consider it also one of the easiest ways to give opportunities both for choice and for concentration. Since in my experience—not Montessori's—reading developed before writing, I shall postpone any discussion of this use of insets and assume that you have provided yourself with a form-board. If, however, you wish to make your own set, turn to the section "Resources" in the appendix.

The first thing to do is to play with the form-board yourself, before you let baby see it. You'll find which shapes fit in most easily, which may need a touch of sandpaper, which, if any of them, can be fitted into a space it shouldn't be in. Now decide what names you are going to use for each shape. Circle, square and triangle are obvious; will you say semi-circle or half-circle, if there is one? Crescent? Oval or ellipse? The important thing is to be consistent. The name matters, because your child is certainly remembering names even if she is not saying them just yet, and identifying these simple shapes by name leads smoothly into matching sounds to letters.

Now, decide which two you are going to offer first; let's say, circle and half-circle. Put all the rest safely away. Find a time, probably in the morning (housework shouldn't have priority) when the small person is in good-humour, not hungry, not tired. Have some other amusement at hand—perhaps the trowel for digging in the garden. This is as much for your sake as hers: to get you into the habit of giving a choice.

Sit down on the floor together, produce the new object, take out the two insets and put them back; then take them out and try to persuade her to feel them round their edges. If that works, you may be able to get her to feel around inside the openings, but I confess that I have never been able to get either children or grandchildren to go through this part of Montessori's routine.

More likely she'll grab both insets and try to shove them in anywhere, hit and miss. That's alright; she has the idea and she'll soon find which is which. If she doesn't try, just wants to eat them or throw them away, she's not yet ready for this contribution, so you put the whole thing away for a few weeks, without fussing. (I know that babies putting things in their mouths are trying to find out what they are, but it's not going to give any useful information about insets.)

If she does try to use them more or less correctly—especially if she puts them in place right away—it's time to use the first two of the Three Steps, giving her each in turn and saying:

Circle; circle.(put this in place)
Half-circle; half-circle.(put this in)

Then,

which is circle? Which is *half*-circle?

If you have been playing the same game with socks and shoes she knows what you are looking for. And, for the same reason, you know whether she's ready to be interested or not. Suppose she's taking them out and putting them in with satisfaction, but didn't get the names right; let her practise. Then, when she's finished, repeat the words as you pack up and put the board away. The next day give square and circle instead, see if she gets those names correctly.

If you are using wooden or plastic insets each shape will have its own square frame, so you offer a selected pair at a time. As I said in the case of the form-board, make sure that neither of the pair you are offering can fit inside the space for the other, a triangle inside a circle, for instance. Then, you have to place them on something that contrasts in colour, so that the shape of the space to be filled shows up clearly. A coloured tray will do, or, best for the plastic insets, a neat length of heavy fabric on which they are less likely to slip around.

As you know, children develop at different rates. You may have one who can pop everything in position but does not respond to names. Save up the board for a little later and play more games with those two steps. It would be a pity if he tired of the board before learning to attach a specific sound to at least a few abstract shapes. Perhaps you can get one of those similar toys where pictures of cars and buses are the moveable objects. There are three more or less distinct abilities being fostered: one, dexterity—hand and eye co-ordination; two, concentration; three, attaching sounds to abstract shapes, to prepare for identifying letters.

So I should add that it would not be remarkable if your child should discover letters and want to identify them without any of this preparation, but that this more likely with a second or third child who sees letters in use. (That's what happened with our second.)

This is where the Third Step is reached. With the first two you were just asking to have the two objects pointed out. Then baby begins to speak. You try the sequence:

Apple. Apple. Banana. Banana.
Show me apple? Show me banana?

What's this? "Ap"
And what's this? "Nana"

"That's right. What a good, clever girl you are!"
A hug and, probably, some banana. If it's not
eating time, use a book and a box, any two objects
whose names you already know she recognises.

So, transferring this third step to the form
board, you may find yourself with a pupil who can
name everything but who doesn't find it easy to
turn the pieces round the right way to fit in. Keep
the board as one of the options for "lessons," but do
not hesitate to offer letters.

Another reason for reading this chapter in good
time: you need a supply of solid, three-dimensional
CAPITAL letters, made from plastic or wood, or, if
you have not been able to buy these, made by
yourself from play-dough and baked in a slow
oven. Why capitals? You'll find an explanation in
the second section.

I had so much trouble, after publication of
Anything School Can Do . . ., responding to
requests for sources of supply that I will only say
that supplies of plastic capitals are strangely
variable. The best set I have known came with a
Fisher-Price desk; the magnetised letters fitted
individually, in alphabetical order, into a moulded
tray which slid in underneath the desk. At times
here in Dublin every little stationer's shop has for
sale cheap packages from China with quite
satisfactory letters; at other times they vanish.
Better than these, larger and more solid, much
cheaper than Fisher-Price, are the set we are
using now, bought in Evans of Mary's Abbey,
Dublin 1. Watch out for sets in which the letter O

27

is almost square, Q and S angled to correspond; avoid this.

The better toy shops may have an alphabet cut out in plywood, letters about 2½ inches tall. If you have found a fret-saw to make the insets (see Resources) you could make letters also. For these it's well to have good models. I suggest the complete alphabet from Marion Richardson's *Writing and Writing Patterns,* but if I were cutting an alphabet based on these I would make the outer lines of M go straight up and down, so that, in the hand, it can be distinguished from W. In some of the plastic sets N is very much the same as Z, but even the child who pointed this out wasn't confused; Z is so rarely used, and so clearly identified with ZOO.

While you are collecting insets and letters and some other structured material—the nesting cups, for example—you had better decide where you mean to store them. Just as you have to find a secure lock-up to keep even slightly dangerous cleaning materials out of baby's reach, you need to arrange one or two shelves that can be reached, where these few special "lesson" things can be kept in order. It will not do to dump them all into a basket. The way in which you store each set, the nesting cups nested in order, the insets in their own box or tray, is part of your child's education. You will find your care rewarded, because somewhere between one and two almost all children become very interested in putting things in the right place. That's why you need to work out what the right place is. I never found it difficult to be patient, or to find time, or to deal with any of the other problems that people raise.

28

Orderly storage was my biggest difficulty, as new material accumulated. My most satisfactory solution was a three-tier trolley; just a suggestion.

In the next chapter I describe work with the materials you have assembled.

3

Letters, Then Words

Now we are considering a small person, aged probably between eighteen and twenty-eight months, who is picking up new words at the rate of three or four a day, very likely more, because we are delighted about the first few words but we soon lose track. (Just once I managed to write down most of the words used by one of my sons on his second birthday and the day after it; two hundred, which I gather is not a large vocabulary for that age.)

Your pupil has come to accept the custom that you show him two things, tell him their names, and then ask him to give or show you one of them, even though you can see them and could perfectly easily pick one up yourself, and that then you ask him what each one is.

Incidentally, it's not important that he say "pentagon" or "rectangle" when you're playing Three Steps with the geometrical insets; if he can recognise your names for half-a-dozen of these objects and produce any recognisable response, it's time to introduce letters. You have provided an alphabet, or better still, two alphabets, at any rate some extra vowels, of CAPITAL letters which can be picked up, felt and moved around. You have taken care that the future student has not seen the letters. They are going to be presented two at a time.

But how are they going to be named?

Not Ay, Bee, See, Dee. Discussion can be found in the second half, in the section, "Identified phonically." So, before you offer anything you have to become familiar with the sounds you are going to use, which are, of course, the sounds you think of when you are mentally pronouncing a word that you have not met before. If they seem unfamiliar, it is only in the context of reciting the alphabet. In English, because the language has grown up from so many different sources, some letters signify many different sounds. To make the way smooth for the beginner, as it is for Finnish and most other children, we select just one sound for each letter; the most frequent and most satisfactory for our purpose are the sounds most often met in words of one syllable: short vowels (A,E,I,O,U) and "hard" consonants. Here is a list:

at bag cup dip egg fun hug it
jump kiss leg man pop quix
run snap tap van wet yes zip.

I am sure you understand that you give A the sound it has in "at", B the sound in "bag," and so on. These are the most frequent sounds anyway.

If the words *Granny, Teddy, Daddy or Mummy* are important in your household you will have to break the news early on that some letters have more than one sound; Y has one sound at the beginning of a word, another at the end. The sound of the final letter of the previous paragraph is one of those things which we allow ourselves to ignore for the moment.

Next, you think for a moment about simple words that your learner knows and likes. Suppose she has a brush she is fond of; that won't do, because "SH" is a distinct phonogram that has to wait.

My current grandchild has a large dice. This would not do at all, because neither the "I" nor the "C" nor the silent "E" correspond with the letters you are going to introduce.

Let's suppose that DADA, BUS, HAND, PLUG, BAG, SOCK suggest themselves. I propose these because you'll be able to have the actual things at hand when the time comes. If you think far enough ahead you can give to favourite toys names that will be helpful at this stage; you might have a kangaroo with baby, KANGA and ROO, as in the Pooh books. You have an alphabet, whether plastic or wood. Sort out the letters that make of the words you have decided on: B,U,S,H, N,P,L,G, with two As and two Ds if you intend to make DADA—two Ms may be needed instead— and put them in suitable small box. Hide the rest of the alphabet for the present. Best would be three boxes, one for the two letters you mean to present first, another for the set that make some familiar words, a third treasure chest from which you will gradually dole out extra letters when the initial eight or ten are thoroughly familiar.

By now you will know the most fruitful time for "lessons", probably in the morning. You offer a choice, "Would you like to play with your nesting cups, or would you like to know about letters?" showing two of them. It would be very surprising if the new alternative were not chosen. So you produce U and P, give her U, encourage her to feel

32

the shape, put it down and say "Uh."

Then do the same with P, then, as usual, ask to be shown P, then U, then ask what each of them are.

Remember, if she doesn't get them right, don't look disappointed, just say again what they are, put them away and move on to the next thing, cooking or painting or whatever. Wait a few days and try again.

But it's rather more likely that there will be an immediate demand for more letters. I've come across accounts in several different books of children aged about two who found capital letters and who insisted on being told most of the alphabet right away. The Montessori-trained mother in Michael Deakin's *The Children on the Hill* intended to make sandpaper letters but her two-and-a-half year old son spotted plastic capitals in a shop window, persuaded her to buy them and, it seems, knew half of them by evening and had begun to make words. It is in case your child is specially eager that I have suggested you have more than two letters available, but that you keep at least half the alphabet out of sight; you know by now how very persuasive a nearly-two-year-old can be when he has guessed that there are further supplies of toy animals or biscuits or biros within reach; but twenty-six letters all at once are too much .

It could be that for countless generations parents have shown their children, at just the age I have in mind, how to recognise edible seeds, how to distinguish the tracks of a deer from those of a dog. Whatever the reason, children at this age are brighter than we usually give them credit for being.

So, use your own judgement. Take out further pairs of letters as long as the magic lasts, but put them away before your child is tired or confused; say, "We'll have letters again to-morrow."

You can, and to my mind should, move from letters to words well before the child knows the whole alphabet. The reason for learning them is to get at words. Once the relationship is clear there will be a stronger motivation to learn the rest of the letters, while once some letters are recognised within familiar words there is little danger of forgetting them or becoming confused.

As to how you go about it, just be alert to your child's interest. It was from my eldest boy that I learnt how to help the others—when I wasn't foolishly following expert instructions. (See introduction). So here I shall recount how he made the jump between letters and words, shortly after his second birthday.

The two of us were kneeling on the floor just inside the door of the livingroom. If it had been "lesson time" we would have been using a table, or sitting on a rug, so this must have been a moment of unplanned enthusiasm. We had between us a blank sheet of paper, I had a pencil.

I draw large D. He says "Duh". I draw A. He says "Ah."

I point rapidly at first the one, then the other; he says "Da."

I ask excitedly, "What did you say? Da?"

At once I write the rest of DADA and he says the whole word. Once Alasdar had grasped the idea of "blending" letters it was simply a matter of giving him more letters and thinking of the right words to keep him happy. For him I hadn't even got 3-D letters, whether of wood or plastic; we were using the quite unattractive small sandpaper letters I had made. The other Early 3-D children had the advantage of moveable letters, so that I could move M U G closer and closer together, MU G, MUG, while just chancing to have the student's own mug somewhere in sight.

Some people insist that it is not possible to "sound" letters, that you have to teach "Ba, be, bi, bo, bu," then "Da, de, di, do, du," and so on. I understand that Japanese mothers have to go through some such scheme, but not only is it needless for English speakers, it could create problems. How do you pronounce Ca(t), Ce(dar), Ci(rcle), Co(at), Cu(p)? My way, you can have CAT and COAT and CUP and postpone Cedar and Circle until the reader can read so well that context, combined with growing knowledge of the world, will make it easy to guess what they mean.

I have read that Japanese mothers, as a matter of course, teach their children to read the seventy-two-character syllabic "alphabet" before they start school, and that problems in connection with reading are very rare. Twice I asked Japanese men if this were so, but they could not tell me.

Recently I found myself on a long journey sitting with a Japanese mother of two small boys, so I asked her. This time we spoke Esperanto, so we understood one another. She said this was indeed the ordinary custom. If the men could not answer, it may have been because men spend so little time at home that they do not know what is going on, and of course most of us forget our own early years.

35

English does set more obstacles in the way of the young reader than do many other languages. Esperanto, which is completely phonetic, makes an enlightening contrast. But it is because English presents such problems that early help is desirable.

A short break here for clarification. Two or three times now I have mentioned "lessons" or "lesson time." I have put the words in inverted commas, because I do not mean a set time, nor a routine resembling school. I mean simply that the children passed their time in many different ways, probably learning something new all the time, out in the garden or helping in the kitchen, and *to them* fitting insets was probably all of a piece with putting away spoons and forks or riding the rocking horse. The distinction between the orderly Montessori-style activities, when I would have a choice available and ask, "Do you want to do some insets first or would you like to do some sewing?" and time spent painting with poster colours on the tiled kitchen wall was in my mind only, and not very clear there. (Sewing meant using a blunt carpet-needle to go around holes in pictures they had drawn themselves on a postcard; "doing insets" would mean filling in with pencil lines outlines which they had drawn with their geometrical insets.)

Now, sorting spoons and forks into sets is a sort of mathematical activity, but I never counted it as "lessons." Painting helps writing, but as far as I was concerned it was an end in itself. Possibly "lessons" were planned steps toward reading, writing and maths which fostered concentration and which were usually suggested by me, but that

36

does not cover Montessori's exercises in balance, the sense of weight, the sense of touch which I would from time to time fit in among the choices. Only last week I was surprised to be told by my sculptor daughter, now in her thirties, that she clearly remembers, and values, the game of matching different fabrics by feeling them with her eyes closed, or even blindfold. If you want to know more about such activities, borrow one of Montessori's books from the library. The aspect I want to stress now is that I tended to suggest such things early in the day, so in that sense there might be "lesson time"; secondly, that they usually took very little time and the day's "work" would as often as not be finished by ten o'clock; thirdly, the child always had the third option, of going away and amusing herself in some other way. Remember, *The child must always be free to take it or leave it alone.*

In practice, one of the children would quite likely take both suggestions. Then sometimes they might become so absorbed in something that they would continue for ages. Quite often they would come to me first, knowing what they wanted to do, especially when they had "cracked the code" of reading, and would bring along a book at any time, "Listen to me reading."

So now you know what I mean by "lessons." If you are tempted to say that you'd never have time for all that, note some of the findings of the five-year Oxford Pre-School Research Project, run by Professor Jerome Bruner. He told us here in Dublin that good childcare was *that style of care that increases the child's capacity to manage its own attention* and that this is best done by activities that have a goal, that give the child feedback, so that she knows what she is doing and that *when children were encouraged to do something that really stretched their minds they tended to go off on their own to do something of the same order*.

This is just what I found long before I heard Bruner speak.

In the morning we would combine washing up with plans for work. Then an hour so of activity, one thing leading to another, the current baby in its basket or fastened in its chair with a something to do, so that it wouldn't distract the others. I might spend some time with one, go off and do some housework, bringing baby with me, come back to see how things were going and "lessons" would be over. But for the rest of the day all the children would be busy. They might need my help, to mix paints or to listen to them, I might need theirs to sweep the stairs or pick up stuff in their rooms, but I have no doubt at all that the time spent in organising work for them was saved over and over again.

This interruption is not accidental. While I am trying to give a clear account of one straight-forward way of helping children to read, I feel it's important to put it in perspective. It seems to me that if I were to list first move, second move, third move, parents might feel that one step should follow the other every few weeks and that these should be the principal activities in a child's life. These paragraphs are meant both to slow things down and to suggest that your child will be reading, with your help, but not to-morrow.

Practical instructions had come to the point where you were using movable letters to make the names of familiar objects—or familiar actions, like JUMP, HUG, KISS. I said that letters have significance because of words and I had already suggested how you can find out whether baby has grasped what some words mean. I have also implied that using words for pleasure, in nursery rhymes and songs is essential; it's more than a preparation for reading, it's sharing in the life of generations.

The next essential for reading is reading. I said you would find a good deal of what I have to say familiar. Nothing, I should think, is more familiar than the advice to read to and with your children.

Go to the local library if you have one within reach. Ask relatives to give books or book tokens even as christening presents. Once the children are ready to listen they need a good supply. Some books they will want to hear over and over again, so I suggest that, for self protection, you don't read anything that you don't enjoy yourself. I hesitate to suggest any titles, because so often the little books which our children especially enjoyed, like the Epaminondas books or *Huff the Hedgehog* are out of print.

Of course the books from which you read are in lower case. I don't know of anything in capitals except the Asterix books; very much enjoyed long before the child can catch the point of half the jokes—that's how one learns. I shall be discussing home-made books, but you may already have noticed that we are helping to bridge the gap by printing some familiar and less familiar rhymes in large capitals at the end of this book. These may prompt you to introduce some of the words.

It probably seems that I have left you very

short of suggestions for words you can make with the movable letters. Really, that can't be helped because there is no point in making words that your almost-reader doesn't know in real life, and only you know what's available. In chapter four I intend to describe our next step, the picture cards, and for these I make quite a few suggestions which may fit in at the earlier stage. So long as the student is enjoying the letters there's no need to rush on to cards, though it would be wise to start making them ahead of time, otherwise you'll find yourself sitting up late at night trying to have a new set ready for the morning. Meanwhile word-building—that is making new words by changing just one letter—may turn out to be an acceptable game, in which you explain unknown words, or try to explain that some proposals, like FUMP simply don't have any meaning in English. The possibles are: LUMP, MUMPS, RUMP, BUMP, PUMP, SUMP, HUMP, JUMP. I had a feeling that TUMP might mean something; it does: a mound made around the trunk of a tree.

Then, BELL, FELL, DELL, HELL. Better not mention the last one, it's amazing how children can fix on it.

BEND, FEND, FENDER, REND, LEND, MEND, TEND.

BEST, JEST, JESTER, NEST, REST, PEST, LEST.

RUST, CRUST, DUST, DUSTER, BUST, JUST, GUST.

Since C and K sound the same at this stage—you have not introduced the "soft" C— words ending in CK don't present a problem: PICK, LICK, SICK, BRICK, STICK, WICK,

TRICK.

There are possibilities for a good deal of fun while explaining some of these, provided you manage to think up explanations. If it's not fun, forget it. You will find that the cards can give as much practice as may be needed.

4

Reading What You Know

Now for the cards. When you have made some you will know when it's time to produce them. It surprises me that cards like these are not produced commercially; I have seen several different reading aids, but each seems to lack something. Often you find pictures and words but no control. Sometimes word and picture are attached like a jig-saw, so that only the correct word will fit, but this removes the possibility of checking for oneself. But it is just as well that sets like these are not on the market; if you have to manufacture your own, they will match your own child's interests.

This means you have to draw your own pictures. Don't worry. A child of three, or less, is not fussy about appearances. All that matters is to draw something that suggests the object, and to draw two the same. You need some packs of postcards or a larger pack of correspondence cards, a good big pack of fibre-tips in different colours, some free time and a selection of suitable words.

In the example I give here we have PEG, FAN,

JUG, PIN, BOX, PAN.

Collect a jug that is often seen on the table. If drawing comes easily, just draw it on the upper three-quarters of one of the cards, then do the same on another. If otherwise, try it out a few times on scrap paper, so that you draw something that more or less fills the space. Even a baby may

be puzzled by a half-inch jug in the middle of a three-inch square.

We used a fan because it is mine and the children knew it well. Get a real clothes peg and look at it carefully while drawing. There is nothing else like it, so it's easy to recognise. No harm in using a ruler if you need one. Make a note to bring baby out to hang up and collect washing and to say quite often, "Will you pick up the peg, please."

The pin I have drawn is a nappy pin; this is copied from a real set; it is only at the moment of writing that I have realised that nappy-pins are probably obsolete. Rather a pity; disposable nappies are simple to use, but not simple to dispose of in the long run. You had better use an ordinary safety-pin, or I suppose you could stick a straight pin onto a card, or draw a pen instead—but who uses pens now?

The problem is that PIN and PAN are intended to resemble each other. We usually included something of the sort in every set, and it's not easy to find alternatives here; JAG to resemble JUG? FIN to resemble FAN? Two of the former, cut from advertisements, would do if your child is very sophisticated in respect of cars, while the latter would be OK if you often prepare fish.

Note that it would be all right to include real objects, or bits from advertisements, along with drawings, so long as they are a pair, but I think you'll find that drawing is much quicker than hunting up matching pictures.

When all the pictures (or things) have been completed, go back to the scrap paper and practise writing the words so that the letters will be the same height. There's a model alphabet at the end of this chapter. Next, write the appropriate words in large letters in the lower quarter of each card. Then neatly cut off one of the words of each pair, put the whole collection in an envelope and write all the words on the outside.

I have told how Alasdar first read DADA. If I recount how he used the first cards you will understand their possibilities.

He (aged about two-and-a-half) was given the set of complete cards, that is, the set with both pictures and words and encouraged to set them out on the floor side by side. Then one picture was placed under the card it matched and he was given the rest of the pictures. Would he guess that he was expected to put them in place? He did.

Next thing was to give him one of the words, suggest he might read it. It said FAN. Where would it go? He put it under the picture of the fan. Then I was inspired to start a routine which turned out to be decidedly helpful: I picked up FAN and showed him that it matched, letter for letter, the word on the complete card in the top row. The result was that if he were to put PIN under PAN he would see *for himself* that he had made a mistake and would be easily able to correct it. This meant that he could use his ability to read "whole words" as soon as he developed it, but would still depend on the reliability of phonics.

The long-term advantage was that all the children who learnt in this way were very sound on spelling.

Incidentally, there's room for a warning on spelling. If adults want to take part in spelling bees, let them look after themselves. As you will see in the second section of this book, knowing the names of letters does nothing to support reading development; similarly, calling out those names in sequence has only a remote relationship with being able to do what is required—write them correctly. If you want to check children's ability to spell, get them to write the words down.

This game seems to have been exactly right for Alasdar at the time. He continued to play it with care and attention for months, which meant that his father and mother had to work fairly hard after his bedtime to keep up supplies. Of course each set was kept in its own envelope, with the words written on the outside.

Before long we extended the use of the cards

by a more advanced version of the game, in which the pictures without words were set out, words matched to them, and the result checked by referring to the complete card.

One early set was EGG, CUP, GUN, VAN, BUS. In self-defence, I want to say that the gun we depicted was a nice little cap-gun less than three inches long, a toy of my husband's. Then we used HAT, COT, PEG, PIG, POD. The models, apart from the pig, were all around the house, the peg not a clothes peg but one he used to hang up his coat.

OO seemed the best way to introduce letter combinations. ZOO is a word that crops up in books as well as in advertisements in buses. I remember we used Alasdar's own three-legged STOOL, the MOON, a SPOON, a HOOP and, for control, a picture of a small boy trying to HOP.

Finding that OO was acceptable, we moved on to OW: their father had made a toy town for the children and a picture of that worked well; we added OWL, TOWER, COW, BROW. If that seems lost without eyes, you could try drawing a FROWN.

Next came a set that proved to be a favourite. We drew the children's own clothes, DRESS, SKIRT, SHIRT, SOCK, SANDAL, COAT.

We did not notice at the time that COAT has "OA" with a sound that is neither O nor OO, but since the readers didn't notice either it was all to the good. You have to be prepared to chance your arm with English spelling.

We realised that the "SH" in SHIRT was new; it was accepted because the garment was recognised. A picture of finger on lips for SH, then

SHIP, SHOP, DISH, BRUSH, SPLASH. The CHURCH from the toy town was given ARCH of toy blocks, CHAIR, WITCH, CLOCK and STICK for company.

EE and EA were introduced together, with GREEN, LEAF, TREE, BEAN, SEAT, DEER.

There was a quickly made set in which the cards had different coloured squares of gummed paper and I don't think anyone noticed that the OW at the end of YELLOW did not sound quite like COW. I remember drawing apples and bananas, so I suppose I must have used ORANGE to explain that G sometimes sounded differently.

Alasdar played with these for months. He would take one envelope, come back for another, and only when he had five or six sets laid out on the floor would he come to me for quality control. Rarely was there a mistake; if there were, I might let it pass, or I might suggest that he look again at, perhaps, ship and shop.

However, the cards did not by any means take up all his time. There were games of carrying a glass of water without spilling a drop, there were balls and blocks, plenty of these, made from hardwood offcuts, there were fires to be made, sticks collected, peas podded, pencils and paint, beads to be matched with numbers, cars to be driven through the toy town, cog-wheels to interlock, his rocking horse to ride and care for, the garden and the whole hillside to explore. There was also a solid block of reading at bedtime and odd bits on demand through the day.

So perhaps his next step is not so surprising, though it did surprise me at the time. His father found a *First Reader* published in Ireland. There was a picture of a 44 bus, the Enniskerry bus, a picture of hay-making, something on every page. The print was large and clear and there were only one or two sentences per page. The snag was that the print was in lower case, and he had been shown only capitals.

He must have been absorbing more than we realised when we were reading to him because he sat on my knee to read that book and wouldn't give up, apart from a break for lunch, until he had finished it. The only word that puzzled him was "HIGH"; the people in the picture had hayforks and they were tossing the hay high in the air. He was then three-and-a-quarter.

The second book in that series had not yet been published, so Sean looked around and found *Beacon Readers*, which I have mentioned in the introduction. They had good stories and they had those useful phonic tables, matched with the stories, at the end of the book. Over the years the children, at least the Early 3-D Phonic children, would come to me at any time in the day and ask me to listen to them reading. I would turn to the appropriate page at the back, take them through a short list, and then we would turn to the story. This stage usually lasted about six weeks, then they realised that they could read silently, they didn't need anyone to listen.

Even so, I would often propose reading as an option when deciding on the morning's work, probably in order to keep their stage in the phonic lists—we called them "the back of the book"— level with the story they had reached; the children could not be expected to check on this for themselves. Once the early stages were over it may have been unnecessary; when Pierce was going on for six I said to him one day, "We don't seem to have done any 'back of the book' for ages. Try this page and I'll help you with the hard ones."

"Which hard ones? Symphony? Determination?"

For which reason I say, if you can find a reading series with decent content, not Mammy or Mummy at the sink, Daddy washing the car, boy up a tree, sister standing beneath lost in admiration, both of them stuffing themselves with sweets and cakes, but instead good pictures and mildly amusing stories, carefully planned to introduce new letter-clusters in an orderly way, well, it will save you some trouble. (See Resources.) If the only things that come your way are as ghastly as some that are being used in schools now, just carry on reading books that you both enjoy and letting the children take part. The cards make clear the essentials on which they can build for themselves.

The first sets of cards which I have described do not do everything. I realised that it was a bit of luck that Alasdar found he could read lower-case text when he had been shown nothing but capitals, so when the succeeding children were managing well with cards in capitals I began to add the same words in lower case tucked in under the capitals. At the same time I explained that for centuries all writing was in capitals; lower case and cursive (handwriting) had developed when people wanted to write capitals in a hurry.

I made a few cards showing all three forms of the letters that look different: O and o are the same, t close enough to T, but the relationship between e and E needs to be demonstrated; the children were all tracing from books of Writing Patterns; they found this information acceptable. You will find a discussion of capitals and lower case in the second half of this book.

It seems to me that there is just one hump to be got over once children have learnt to associate a certain sound with one letter, and then gone on to blend these sounds. As I said, Finns and Spaniards never meet this hump. I am not sure that anyone else does. Many languages have different sounds for letter clusters, as we have sounds for CH which do not relate either to C or H. Children seem to learn these quite easily, provided that they are introduced gradually. The hump is the effect of a final E (or Y) on a vowel that comes in the earlier part of the word: HAT, HATE; HID, HIDE; HOP, HOPE; HUG, HUGE. It is the convenience of having this hump as it were smoothed out for you that makes a reading series tempting. If you haven't got one you had better clear the air once your child has been puzzled a few times. If you can persuade her to go back to word-making with the movable letters you'll soon make the pattern clear. When she is reading to you and pauses, you can say "look", pointing to the final e, then, pointing to the varying vowel, "is this U (uh) or (you)?"

If she's finding this annoying, just put in the right word and let her get on with the story. Sometime you can go through nursery rhymes that she reads readily because they are familiar and point out one or two examples,

"Little Boy *Blue*,
Come blow your horn . . ."

down to the last line, "He's *sure* to cry" and show her that she really knows the trick already, it's just a matter of getting used to it.

Almost every other word in this rhyme is straightforward; "WHERE" and "WILL" come near enough to the sound you have given for W in WET. In fact most of the set, WHERE, WHY, WHAT, WHO are "sight words"; "WHERE" does not match "HERE" nor does "WHAT" match "HAT" while the "Y" of "WHY" does not obey the rule you have given. If your reader doesn't notice it, don't remark it; I believe it to be a mistake to base reading on "sight words," but one cannot read English without absorbing a good few.

"WAKE" in "Will you wake him?" provides an example of the long sound of A.

> Ladybird, ladybird,
> Fly away home.
> Your house is on fire,
> And your children are gone.
> All except one
> And that's little Ann,
> And she has crept under
> The frying pan.

has a helpful mix of long and short A, O and I; the word I would pass without comment would be "ALL". I have just noticed that "GONE" sounds like "GON"; well, "SON" rhymes with "SUN", but this observation reminds me that I've never noticed "GONE" before, which means that when children are three-quarters of the way to independent reading they select whichever option makes sense.

However, you do not have to shift straight from cards to nursery-rhymes in capitals, provided within these covers, or to reading in lower case. One of the most enjoyable stages in the process of reading instruction is that of making your own books, so that your child can move smoothly from matching cards to "reading for meaning." Several of our books have survived, worn but legible. They are worn, not because they were read very frequently, there was no need for that, but because each child had his or her own book, so once it was familiar the blank pages were used for drawing.

Model Alphabet

A B C D E F G
H I J K L M N
O P Q R S T U V
W X Y Z

5

Making Your Own Book

For the kind of book I have in mind the best material is a spiral-back sketchbook of cartridge paper. It needs to be sturdy to stand up to repeated use and you will find the cartridge paper more agreeable for writing and drawing than anything lighter. The drawings reproduced here were on pages seven inches by five which means that they have been reduced; they were drawn by an elder sister aged about thirteen. Having discovered that they photo-copy satisfactorily I have decided that an authentic book, with comments, will suit our purpose better than description or instructions.

SAND IS
IN HIS
SANDAL

SAND IS
IN HIS
BED

This was Killian's book; there are traces of a page which probably indicated how he came to have sand in his sandal. Note that it is based on fact, and that he would have met SANDAL and BED on picture cards; this makes the connection by IN, IS, HIS.

MAMA
HAS
A
DUST PAN
AND A SWEEPING BRUSH

HAS is close to HIS. You may have noticed that S in words like this sounds more like Z; no need to mention it. The ING of sweeping is taken for granted once SWEEP has been made out, but it could be a cue for making lots of words ending in ING.

Note that when this was made Mama probably hadn't got a vacuum cleaner. The first one I had was an awkward brute, not suited to a four-year-old, and anyway VACUUM is a word out on its own, not needed by young readers. HOOVER would be fine, if that's what you say.

KILLIAN HAS
A
SWEEPING
BRUSH.

HE SWEEPS
AND GETS A PENNY

(Comment here; that penny surprises me. I
don't remember paying children for ordinary
jobs.)

But the final Y of PENNY appears several
times in the next two:

KILLIAN CAN JUMP

THE KANGAROO
CAN JUMP

BARNEY CAN
NOT JUMP

BARNEY IS A PUP

KILLIAN IS A BOY

EOIN IS A BABY

Immediately before that is a double-page spread in which Killian and the kangaroo see each other, so I suspect a visit to the zoo. It may be simply that kangaroo is a good long word that gives a feeling of achievement.

Then a page related to the cards with colours and fruit:

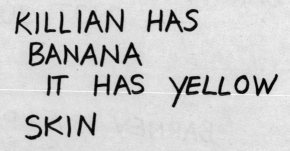

KILLIAN HAS
BANANA
IT HAS YELLOW
SKIN

ALISON HAS
A RED
APPLE

Then there is another fruit, with a suggestion
that SH needs practice,

PIERCE
PUTS
LEMON
   ON   HIS   FISH

SH SH SH

So, the next two pages have three mushrooms:

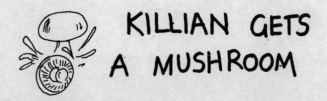 KILLIAN GETS
A MUSHROOM

HE PUTS IT
IN THE PAN

Some readers may feel that they are getting too
much of Killian's book. The text is not very
exciting. But I hope it's clear that it's not meant to
be copied, or shown to your own children unless
they are curious. It is an example of how one can
write records of everyday activity, combining
them with reading cards and adding "letter
clusters" gradually.

DADA HAS THE MUSHROOM FOR DINNER

DADA LIKES KILLIAN'S MUSHROOM

Here we have "LIKES" with a long sound for I, and a real novelty, an apostrophe S for KILLIAN'S.

Now come the last two pages of reading in capitals:

KILLIAN
CAN GET UP
THE TREE

In the final page I find, now, that I made a mistake. I wrote, EOIN CAN NOT GET UP, HE CAN JUST LOOK. That sounds so like a reading book. We don't say "CAN NOT" in a context of that sort, it should have been "CAN'T." After all, we had had an apostrophe.

EOIN CAN NOT GET UP
HE CAN JUST LOOK

Those few pages, which may have covered a couple of weeks, lead to one in large lowercase,

Dada is sick, Eoin is sick, Killy isn't sick, he is well. The doctor came.

And after, presumably, a few day's distraction with a sick baby, the satisfactory information, in lower case that's not much larger than ordinary print,

Now Killian can read

about Cock Robin

and the Sparrow

and the Beetle

and the Owl

and the Lark.

It is clear to me now that a future birdwatcher had identified a nursery rhyme that he thought worth reading; his adult career consists in drawing and writing about birds. This book seems to belong to the year when he was four. He didn't bother to read until he was five, when he found that there were books as well as rhymes about birds. Then, when he was seven, Dada's Birthday Book, a valuable record, has :

I found a hedgesparrow's nest. The first day I found it there were no eggs in it and the next day I looked in it and there was one egg and it was blue. And now there are four eggs in it. And it is a very neat nest made of feathers and moss. Then I found a blackbird's nest and I often see him on his eggs and they are very big eggs.

In this one can see that he had grasped the use of the possessive apostrophe *s*. His spelling is also competent. He had never been asked to spell eff, ee, ay, tee, haitch, ee, ar, feather; he had read about birds and had met the word "feather" very frequently.

It may be a happy chance that Killian's book is among those that have survived, because of the Early 3D set in the family he was the latest in reaching the ability to read independently. He put in very little time at "lessons." He was outside looking at or waiting for birds from age five or earlier, but it seems to me that that paragraph (which is in a clear cursive hand) shows that without much effort on anyone's part a gradual introduction of shape recognition, capital letter recognition, word-building, reading cards, followed by a demonstration of how we put words together to make sense, provide a base from which a child can take off into reading when he or she feels it worthwhile.

I find that I have similar books belonging to the two youngest boys. Eoin at four (his birthday cake on his fourth birthday is one of the subjects) was reading pages that said: OLIVER likes an EGG for breakfast. DADA likes A CUP OF TEA. Tinu likes RYVITA for breakfast. MAMA made brown BREAD for breakfast.

The difference is that they were collecting sight-words, so not only was "breakfast" repeated, but some words were in capitals, some in lower case, to match the form in which they had learnt them. I had used both so as to give variety. It does not take long in practice to find how many words in lower case look very like each other. However, I have explained in the introduction that this method looked impressive at first but didn't work out so well later.

What I have described here is only the core of the Early Three-Dimensional Phonic Capital approach to reading acquisition. Should Reading Acquisition have capitals too? In the background you must imagine the hum of stories and poems being read to the children, read to them long after they are able to read themselves. Often our bedtime reading session meant that a competent reader was listening while a parent read to the younger ones; if the parent were called away the elder brother or sister would take over.

That was the background. Practice in writing was part of the foreground, and must naturally combine with reading as soon as the reader can handle a brush or pencil. It is a great merit of capital letters that they are relatively fairly easy to write. Oliver at an early age used to write or draw ornamental borders of random letters above some of his pictures. I have found a paragraph ending a review I wrote of a book called *Give Your Child a Superior Mind:*

> Three-year-old beside me has just shown me a letter he had drawn. "You put it in the middle of Barbara's letter and you put S beside it and you have BUS." Then he wrote BUS. Next he showed me a drawing he had made of a man with his mouth open and asked me to tell him to close it. When the man did not obey (Oliver) suggested that I whisper in his ear. It seemed to me that that's how most children think and you'd have to squash them a lot to fit them into the logical pattern of the *Superior Mind.*

He drew these letters rapidly and well. Most days since he was about two and a half he had spent some of "lesson" time filling in ellipses or rectangles drawn with the the help of the geometrical insets that I have described. The filling in at first was erratic, with vague curves aimed in the general direction of the prepared outline. He would have made the outline himself, with a helper holding the template in place. Then he would have been encouraged to put his pencil on the outline, start there, try not to go over the edge at the other end. Any line that could be praised, would be. Next he'd have been encouraged to try to draw the lines straight, and gradually closer together. Coloured pencils, of course.

Just because we might not find this occupation amusing we may suppose that for children it is drudgery. When you watch them it does not seem so. They can quite early understand what their aim is. They themselves can see whether a line has gone over the edge, or not. The better they can control their pencil, the more the satisfaction of mastery; quite young children can be very competent indeed, almost ready to forge banknotes. Result: young people whose hands will do what they want them to do; "hand and eye control", it's called in reviews of education.

The other merits of "doing insets" are the concentration required, and usually evoked, and the language used: inside, outside, in between, almost, straight, crooked, wobbly, heavy, light, shorter, a little longer, thick, thin.

"Just right ! That's a lovely one ! We must keep it."

This is perhaps an interruption in a book in which I am trying to focus on reading, but "doing insets", with the loaded questions, "Which would you like to do first, insets or tracing?" then, "Which would you like to do, a triangle or an ellipse?" was to such an extent a common factor in all the children's learning that it must be mentioned. It all goes together; reading, language, writing, thinking. Remember Bruner, ". . . the style which enables the child to master its own attention."

6

Books for Reading, Now and Later

Once the children have "cracked the code," what use are they going to make of their skill? At first they are going to read the simplest picture-books you can get your hands on and, possibly, a well-planned series, like those *Beacon Readers* we enjoyed or the more modern *Fuzzbuzz* series. You couldn't get anything simpler than the "weather" book I gave to the small grandson who has appeared in these pages from time to time. This is a couple of inches square, with one word and a picture to each opening, rain, sun, hail, wind. I gave it to him just as a toy, but a week ago there was a heavy hailstorm and when he was let out to investigate he repeated the word "hail" as something familiar. His mother told me she had been reading the tiny book with him. He has another picture book which says "Good night" to a roomful of chair, table, bed, teddy and so on, which seems to be a treasure. No suggestion that he is *reading* these, but when he does crack the code these, and his book of nursery rhymes, will meet him more than half way. I mean that when he has made SUN with the plastic letters, perhaps read something about SNOW in his handwritten book, and then finds the little book he used to play with he will discover that he can really read it.

Yesterday an aunt gave him a wildly funny book called *The Princess and the Potty* which we hope will be as useful as it is amusing. Can I tell you where to get any of these? No. In the section on Resources I shall pass on what little information I have about reading series, but picture books tend to have a short shelf-life. (*A Very Hungry Caterpillar* seems to be an exception.) All I can suggest is that you make use of your local library and ask friends to give book-tokens instead of stuffed animals. One real friend in teddy shape is worth a menagerie.

So we come to the important question of what books you collect for reading aloud. I said in the Introduction that some people hold that reading aloud, letting the child see the text, is enough in itself to establish the skill of reading. For some children this is very likely true; the problem is that you do not know whether yours are of that sort or not, so it is prudent to give them some structured assistance. But structure alone without joint enjoyment of poems and stories does not provide much reason for going further once the code has been cracked. The first choice must be books that you loved when you were a child yourself; there is a special sort of sharing in reading those together; you almost feel that there are three people engaged; your child, yourself as reader, and your childhood self. I always remember a gathering of that sort, collecting up to five participants, when my youngest, Oliver,

came to me in the kitchen one morning and asked
me to read him a Pooh story.
I was reading:

> "Whatever's the matter, Piglet?" asked
> Christopher Robin who was just getting up.
> "Heff," said Piglet, breathing so hard that he
> could hardly speak, "a Hell—a Heff—a
> Heffalump"
> "Where?"

I noticed that eldest brother, who, if Oliver was
four, would have been about sixteen, had been
passing through the kitchen, but was now
standing in the doorway. There he stayed until
the end of the story of the Heffalump Pit. If you
don't know it, go and buy *Winnie-the-Pooh* and
The House at Pooh Corner ; the individual stories
are also published as single books, in a larger
format. There used also to be some miniature
editions, boxed. They are for having, not
borrowing. The author is AA Milne, but you will
not need to mention that; I can hardly believe
that any shop selling children's books would not
know Pooh. He has been done into Latin as
Winnie illi Pu. Even the title page makes me
laugh; it shows a charming bust of Pu, a toga on
his shoulders and a laurel wreath on his head,
over the name of the publisher:

Londinii: Sumptibus Methueni et Sociorum
Neo-Eboraci: Sumptibus Duttonis
MCMLXI

(Note: Eboracum was the Roman name for York;
so, New York)

70

A few years ago I was in a bookshop in a small town in Hungary with a Swedish and a Hungarian friend. Kerstin, from Sweden, came over to me and said (in Esperanto, naturally) "Look what I've found for Margareta!" It was Pooh in Hungarian; we recognised the pictures. She bought it and happily presented it; Margareta was grateful but she had to admit that her son had it already.

If, as is very likely, you too have the books already and so don't need to buy them, try to get hold of *The Tao of Pooh*. Eldest daughter gave it to me a few Christmases ago and I tried to buy ten copies to give to all the other family members; the bookshop had only four, and now I don't know who missed out. It is still available. I see from my copy that it was reprinted five times between 1982 and 1985. The author is Benjamin Hoff, the publishers, of course, Methuen.

At this point I shall tell you which other books I have given to the four sets of grandchildren—not counting little Aaron, the one who recognised HAIL. This reminds me to get copies for him and his new brother. In two cases the fact that they have been republished within the last few years suggests that my affection for them was justified; I hope the third will have similar endurance.

I was eleven myself (the date is written on the end-paper) when I found *Celtic Wonder Tales* by Ella Young, with decorations by Maud Gonne. They are about Angus the Ever-Young and the Gobaun Saor and the Dagda Mor, the World Builder, and the coming of the Milesians and the Three Waves that go round Ireland. It enchanted me and I was glad that though most of my other

71

books were gone, I had this to read with my own children. I met two other people of discernment who felt as warmly about it as I did, and I suspect that one of them had some responsibility for getting it republished in Edinburgh. The new edition has impressive information about Ella Young, about how she learnt Irish and gathered these stories from people in her part of the country.

As for *Irish Fairy Tales* by James Stephens, illustrated by Arthur Rackham, I have our own copy beside me, and it is apparent that my husband bought it second-hand—a habit with him; the house is laden with his findings. Nothing in my long experience of reading aloud came to the tongue as creamily as did this. The book fell open at "The Enchanted Cave of Cesh Corran"; I must share a few lines:

"Well !" said Fionn to himself.
"By my hand !" quoth Conan to his own soul.
And the two men stared into the hillside as though what they were looking at was too wonderful to be looked away from.
"Who are they?" said Fionn
"What are they?" Conan gasped.
And they stared again.
For there was a great hole like a doorway in the side of the mound, and in that doorway the daughters of Conaran sat spinning. They had three crooked sticks of holly set up before the cave, and they were reeling yarn off these. But it was enchantment they were weaving.
"One could not call them handsome," said Conan.

"One could," Fionn said, "but it would not be true."

"I cannot see them properly," Fionn complained. "They are hiding behind the holly."

"I would be contented if I could not see them at all," his companion grumbled.

But the Chief insisted.

"I want to make sure that it is whiskers they are wearing."

"Let them wear whiskers or let them not wear them," Conan counselled, "but let us have nothing to do with them."

"One must not be frightened of anything," Fionn stated.

"I am not frightened," Conan explained. "I only want to keep my good opinion of women, and if the three yonder are women, then I feel I shall begin to dislike females from this minute out."

This way of telling the story is not as frightening as the way I met the same story when I was four or five. I remember the picture still, and how anxious it left me about witches; if I were so much as to move a toe in bed one of them would be in and get me.

This book was reprinted a few years ago by Gill and Macmillan so there should be no difficulty in finding it. It must be in most libraries as well.

The third book which I felt I did not want the coming generation to miss is a remarkable creation. I would never have looked at it were it not for an exceptionally laudatory review by Benedict Kiely in *The Irish Times*. A few days after reading it I saw a many-paged hardback with a substantial price. Well, twelve pounds seemed substantial to me. But I was planning to go to England the next day and I would be staying with my daughter in Kent, the mother of the eldest grandson, then aged twelve, and if Benedict Kiely judged well, *The Hounds of the Morrigan* would an acceptable gift. Besides, I could read it on the journey.

It's remarkable because the author, Patricia O'Shea left Galway at the age of seventeen, never returned, never wrote anything until this marvellous mixture, which she spun from her memories and genius when in her forties. You can judge for yourself; it is in paperback, and it is in the library system. There are several copies in my local library.

It made my voyage, by boat and bus, pass like a dream, only dreams are never so funny. The central characters are a boy aged about eight and his brave little sister. She is splendidly independent. The story is self-contained. The time is the present day, but many of the characters encountered by the children will be familiar to readers of the two books I have just been writing about. There is also a memorable frog. Daughter, eldest grandson, and I believe, the other families were as charmed as I was.

The fourth book on general distribution is *The Poolbeg Book of Children's Verse*, edited by Sean McMahon. It is, to my mind, an invaluable intuitive mixture with "The Lady of Shalott" next door to "Fontenoy."

> On Fontenoy, on Fontenoy, like eagles in the
>   sun,
> With bloody plumes the Irish stand, the field
>   is fought and won!

I may have misgivings about making war seem glorious, but they are subdued by the memory of how much I enjoyed both poems myself when young. Tom Moore's "Minstrel Boy" faces "The Burial of Sir John Moore at Corunna", which evens the balance.

In another section are "The Camel's Complaint" and Robert Farren's charming "Colm's Pets"

Colm had a cat
and a wren
and a fly.

(If this gives pleasure, try to get hold of his whole book of poetry about Colmcille, *The First Exile*. There are some delightful verses about the child Colm learning to read.)

The *Poolbeg Book* went on another journey; I brought it with me when travelling to Budapest, on a train that's called the Orient Express, but is not at all like the legend, and I enjoyed every page. It was fun to meet old friends, Ogden Nash's "Isabel" and "The Shooting of Dan McGrew," to meet "Dublin Made Me," which I had never read before, best of all, on St. Patrick's Day, to have the whole of "St. Patrick's Breastplate."

My only warning: don't read aloud page 83, "Be Merry" or Angelo's thoughts about death, from *Measure for Measure* until you have considered your hearers' liability to nightmares. The former is on a page that's blank on the other side and could be removed if that seems prudent.

What I most regret when I look back at the years of learning with the children, is that I did not make more space for poetry. The nursery rhymes, of course, got their share of attention; I

used to recite every thing I knew, Chesterton's
"Lepanto," "St. Crispin's Day," and other rousing
speeches from *Henry V*, a collection of sonnets,
the Creed in Latin, anything to get one
particularly sleepless baby to curl up (later on she
read verse rather well, rather soon) but I did not
encourage the children to learn poems for their
own use and I did not read longer poems with
them as often as I might have. When four or five
of us read "The Pied Piper of Hamelin," sitting on
the grass in the sun in the garden, enjoyment was
evident. Why so rarely? I shall borrow advice that
I met too late; insist that each child choose and
learn by heart one poem per week, to be recited to
the family on Sunday.

There's an obvious bias in my list. You could
call it "Think Irish." Well, I suppose myself to be
writing for Irish readers; others I would expect to
have selections of their own. A little patience, and
you will find that my recommendations are not
insular.

This Irish foundation raises the language
question. First, all I have said in the earlier
chapters about reading acquisition should apply
just as well in an Irish-speaking household—the
same approach is, I believe, being tried out in
parts of Africa. Secondly, even if you are not Irish-
speaking, you have hardly got through school
without meeting some Irish poetry. I grew up in
Gibraltar, taught by Loreto nuns, but I was at
school in Ireland for nearly three terms. I still
remember a fair amount of "Bán chnuic Éireann
Ó" and "Tháinig long O Valparaiso" and "Cad a
dhéanfaimid feasta gan adhmad"—I have
difficulties with spelling, because I was fortunate

enough to meet them before the lovely Gaelic script was banished. I'm just saying, if you know even a little, if you can introduce Irish picture books along with the English ones, do so, so that the language will always be associated with home, not merely with school.

It is up to you to choose from contemporary Irish children's books. When our family was growing up there was nothing like the variety there is now. I know, because over a period of years I used to get bundles of children's books for review and few, apart from Eilis Dillon's, were of Irish origin. Now I am able to give one from time to time when I manage to remember a birthday, but I'm not around to see how the children like them. One report is that Tom McCaughren won over a competent but reluctant reader.

I have assumed that the children we are planning for may be Irish; they are certainly human, and need stories; are likely to be European, and need to know about their roots in Greece; probably Christian, and need to be able to refer back to central figures of the Old Testament if they are to understand much of the New. Even if it's only to have some clues to European painting and the carvings on cathedrals such a background is valuable; if you don't do something to fill it in before the children are nine or ten you may find that you have readers all right, but readers reading exclusively about horses or computers.

It might be convenient if the humanising role of stories were to be met in the Irish ones I have recommended, but the traditional themes tend to be unearthly. The late Bruno Bettelheim, in *The*

Uses of Enchantment proposed that many
contemporary thugs, young and older, are stony-
hearted because their elders failed to lead them
into the human race through folk tales—what we
call fairy stories. Suppose that, when you are very
young, you are told how three sons go to seek
their fortune and two refuse to share their cake
with an old woman who asks for it, or to give a
helping hand to a distressed frog, while the
youngest son listens and assists and then the
elders meet misfortune while the youngest wins
through with the help of the magic acorn the old
woman gave him, well, chances are you will at
least grow up with a notion that it is unwise to
bash old ladies. It is to be hoped that, hearing a
sufficient variety of stories, you will come to
recognise that other people, even frogs, have
feelings that deserve to be taken into account.

So, have a good collection of the stories
collected by the brothers Grimm. Remember that
they were not passed on from adults to children
but told by adults to adults with children
listening in. Many of them can be traced back for
thousands of years, to Egypt and further. My
mother used to tell me the story of a hen called
Old Bun Doon, which her mother used to tell her.
In the Grimm version of the story the mysterious
name is Rumplestiltzkin. This theme is very
widespread, very ancient. Whole books are
written discussing the variations.

Some hold that women on the whole do not get
a fair deal in the traditional stories. I think
Rapunzel, a special favourite here because of a
beautifully illustrated book, is a good enough role
model. You may remember that she was

kidnapped and locked up in a tower by a witch, but she let down her long hair so that a passing prince could use it to climb up to her. She not only outwitted the witch, she turned the tables on her, so that in the end the witch shrunk like withered apple and a crow flew away with her. The prince fell among thorns and lost his sight, but Rapunzel by her tears restored it to him. She took charge, she solved problems and she was loving and loyal.

Then, the Greeks. Not always good role models, but the warp of our culture. *Tanglewood Tales* (Nathaniel Hawthorne) are a classic re-telling, out of copyright, not difficult to find. I would love to see a reprint of *The Story of The Odyssey,* by AJ Church. Probably out of copyright also (mine was published in 1902. *The Spectator* said it was "one of the most beautiful pieces of prose in the English language.") so some publisher may take a hint.

Another book I would love to see in print again is *Tales from Holy Writ* by Helen Waddell. She was a scholar and a poet, author of *The Wandering Scholars* and other enduring books. She told these stories to her nephews and niece, the eldest aged seven,

> for whom the huge umbrella that covered the pony trap was Abraham's tent at Hebron. The background was an old whitewashed house in County Down, its three foot thickness of wall sunk in ivy and in apple orchards, but with the silence of the bog behind it, where at night one could sometimes hear the drumming of the snipe.

Reading them you hear the spoken word; by the time I came to the end of the story of Joseph and his brothers I would be almost in tears myself. Not much point in recommending it if it can't be had, but this book of mine is about beginning reading; Waddell might be back by the time you need her.

We had a series of small books about creation and Abraham and the prophets, brilliant pictures like old stained glass, so much enjoyed that they did not survive and are of course unobtainable now. Most "Bible stories" have habitually had wishy-washy illustrations.

Three sets of books I can recommend wholeheartedly and with the assurance that you will be able to find them. Their appeal is so well recognised that Puffin Books sell them in boxes. It is well to buy, or have someone buy for you, a whole set at once, because then you can be sure of reading them in the correct order, but I cannot decide whether it is wise to let the child or children know you have them.

The three sets are of books by Laura Ingalls Wilder, by E Nesbit and by CS Lewis. The first are recollections from real life of a little girl in a pioneer family gradually moving west in the United States. I don't know whether the word "pioneer" is quite appropriate but the word "family" is. A series remotely based on the books has been shown on television. I looked at one episode and saw that it was altogether inadequate to the simplicity and strength of the original. Just after her seventh birthday our youngest daughter wrote her own account of *The Long Winter*, the first of this series, and in it she referred to events in several of the other books, so it is safe to say they will suit age six and upwards.

The magic Nesbit stories about the Psammead, *Five Children and It* will do very well at the same age: "and upward" means what it says; I must have read them aloud five or six times and continued to enjoy them.

The Narnia stories by CS Lewis should probably wait a little longer, but not too long. To them I should add, a bit later again, his sort-of-SF *Out of the Silent Planet* and *Perelandra*. I had read those when I was about eleven. It was particularly enjoyable to find them again and read them simultaneously with my eleven-year-old eldest son. We read them over three days; I would give him the one I was reading when he came in from school, he'd leave it outside his bedroom door when sleep was taking over at night. Re-reading them as an adult I found that they had made a deep impression on the girl who had read them more than twenty years before.

Never was science fiction more needed than now, when new discoveries come full circle and suggest that the existence of "matter" is doubtful. If you have been accustomed to reading SF yourself, you will agree that Asimov and Clifford Simak and Ursula Le Guin are to be recommended. I don't find recent SF so attractive; it's not just my age, my SF-reading sons say the same; I have noticed that the daughters don't seem inclined to read it; I think they are mistaken.

I must put in a special mention of Harry Harrison, who writes junior SF as well as adult.

The last SF book I enjoyed was Harry's *West of Edeng'*. It is in the adult category, but I passed it on to the eldest grandson; these things enlarge the imagination.

But why special mention of Harry Harrison? Because he is patron of the Esperanto-Asocio de Irlando. I shall not say much about Esperanto here because I have said most of what I want to say in another recent book, *Esperanto for Hope*, but it fits in very well here. If you have found that your child is a competent reader because of your help you will also have found that helping was very satisfying. Esperanto enables you to repeat that satisfying experience, with additions.

An argument that should encourage parents to look into the matter is that research in several countries—Finland, France, Germany etc. has shown that children who learn Esperanto for a year learn other languages more efficiently afterwards. Just now, in Ireland, parents are trying to insist that children should be introduced to European languages other than English in primary school. It is true that children under the age of nine retain some of their infant ability to pick up languages by ear and they reproduce intonation better than they are likely to later on. If they have opportunity to converse with a native speaker of the target language, that is excellent; that's the reason why French and Irish girls are sought after as *au pairs*. There is not the same advantage in being taught, say, French or German at intervals, in a class, by someone who is not a native speaker, much less by someone who has merely done a crash course.

From the point of view of the qualified teacher

at second level, it is no help at all to be faced by a class, some of whom have been taught a little by one method, some a little by another method, while most are normal beginners. (If one or two have lived abroad and have good accents, they can be useful models.)

Now, Esperanto is completely different. There are no irregular verbs, no idioms to memorise. In a very short time you can learn to combine affixes so as to express your ideas correctly, for example, *miaj gepatroj kaj miaj gefratoj eklernas la internacian lingvon,* (my parents and my brothers and sisters are beginning to learn the international language). You could learn it with no help beyond a dictionary (the dictionary in the *Teach Yourself* series contains all the grammar you require in less than thirty pages) and some reading material.

My own book contains a good deal of reading material, with vocabularies, sandwiched into the English text; if you read it, you will be equipped to start teaching your child, or rather, learning along with her. There are many charming children's books in Esperanto published in China. The best is *Pesi Elefanton* (To Weigh an Elephant). A suitable age to begin would be between seven and ten, with a child who is reading comfortably. The fact that Esperanto is completely phonetic is very acceptable. The other fact, that you cannot write a single word in Esperanto without knowing its syntactic role—that is, without having decided whether it is a noun, adjective, verb, adverb, preposition, singular or plural, in the accusative case or not— the fact that doing this seems to come naturally, while the grammar of anything you read is transparent, is what makes Esperanto so very valuable for "language awareness."

It not only helps acquisition of foreign languages, it makes people much more conscious of the structure of their own language. I have often remarked that writers who are renowned for their English style, Newman, Belloc, Churchill, were never taught English; they were taught Latin, and through Latin a sense of the relationships between words spilled over into English. The effect of learning Esperanto is similar, but requires only a small fraction of the time.

I said earlier that you would find that my recommendations were not narrowly nationalistic. It is one of the peculiar merits of Esperanto than translations into it from any national/ethnic language are closer to the tone of the original than translations into some other national language—than, for example, translations into English. Once you have begun to read Esperanto you will have both literature and current affairs of dozens of other peoples within your reach, with some of Asterix as well. You will, in short be doing your child a second good turn.

Finally, don't overlook the nuts and bolts. You taught the sounds of letters rather than their names, but, with one sound or another, people need to know the order of the alphabet. Esperanto will be helpful here, because the dictionary will be used so often.

Let the children know that you, too, need to use an English dictionary from time to time; discussions about the meaning of words should be followed up in the children's presence. Then you can let them see how you use an index, show that a bibliography, where there is one, gives useful suggestions for further reading. If you have Roget's *Thesaurus,* tell them how it works; they are quite likely to get more fun out of it than you do. (And if you have it, please read the final pages of the original introduction, which in current editions is printed at the end.)

I confess that, apart from discussing words and consulting the *Shorter Oxford Dictionary* in public, we did not do these things ourselves. Nobody ever told me to look at a bibliography, it was simply there; if I had thought about it, I would have expected the children to find out for themselves. However, the excellent book by Young and Tyre, *Teach Your Child to Read,* shows that parents can do much more. As well as finding books about the subjects that interest their children, they can outline to them the contents of the book and discuss it afterwards, show what and when to skip, skim and concentrate upon when reading different kinds of material.

It took me years to realise that it was all right to skip. It is, naturally, all right for you to skip the second half of this book if you don't need to be persuaded that it's a good idea to help young children to read.

The Debate about Reading

The Debate

Debates about how and when to teach reading are given much more space than debates about how to teach science or mathematics or art. Quite right too. You cannot get very far with science or maths or literature until you have forgotten about learning to read. I don't say you cannot approach the foothills; it is a good thing to combine the introductions to all these disciplines.

While I write this, in 1990, I learn that science teaching has hitherto assumed that children will normally have reached what the psychologist Piaget called "formal thinking," commonly called abstract reasoning, essential to understanding scientific experiments, by the age of twelve; recent research has shown that many students do not do so until eighteen, while a substantial proportion of adults have never got there at all. The good news is that experiments in cognitive development find that teenagers can be helped to develop in the desired direction.

When I first wrote about teaching reading, in 1965, early reading was not officially acceptable.

"Reading readiness" was supposed to emerge about age six. In 1977 Professor Barbara Tizard of the University of London wrote in the *Times Educational Supplement* about a survey of parent-teacher contact in six nursery schools. It had been found that from 45 to 78 per cent of the parents were teaching the children letters and numbers at home; others would have liked to do so, but were afraid of interfering and confusing the child. The teachers were critical of this activity:

> They thought the parents, instead of starting the children on the 3Rs, should be doing more for them in other directions, through providing stimulating conversation, books and suitable toys.

Reading that, I asked myself, if books were recommended, why banish reading? If jig-saws may be suitable toys, why not letters? And as for stimulating conversation, Barbara Tizard later wrote a significant book, *Young Children Learning, Talking and Thinking at Home and at School*(1984), which demonstrated that conversation at home is commonly far more stimulating than any that occurs in nursery school.

My own *Anything School Can Do, You Can Do Better* was published in Ireland in 1983. In the same year the Open University Press published *Dyslexia or Illiteracy? Realizing the Right to Read*, by Peter Young and Colin Tyre. They said that "dyslexia" as a medical term describing the condition of patients who had formerly been able to read but who had lost this ability because of trauma was clear and useful. When it is defined as:

> a disorder in children, who, despite conventional classroom experience, fail to attain the language skills of reading, writing and spelling commensurate with their intellectual abilities (World Federation of Neurology, 1968) the definition can be seen to be circular: children with difficulties in reading, spelling etc. "fail to attain" reading and spelling skills.

But the passage in that book which I am most pleased to quote is that which concludes, *"The most advantaged children, as far as reading is concerned, are undoubtedly those who learned to read with their parents or family members before or during the early years of schooling."*

The paragraph leading to this conclusion says first that reading, like writing, is an individual and solitary act; no one can read for us, they can only read to us; no one can write for us, they can only write at our dictation or instruction.

Learning to read is an individual act, too, and the best and only way to learn is individually with someone to facilitate the process and to prepare our way and guide us towards the goal. No one can learn for us. To learn we must be motivated and the only satisfactory motivation for learning to read is the motivation to learn to read. Given this motivation, and the cognitive abilities necessary to the learner, the teacher must be supportive, encouraging, and manifest to the learner high expectation of success. This can best be done in the ongoing tasks of reading or writing. If, as parents or teachers, we embark on helping a child to learn to read or write we must be as close to the child and as supportive as if we were teaching the child to ride a bike or to swim. Perhaps the success of any of the models or methods we have discussed are in direct proportion to the extent to which the teachers' skills are used to ensure close contact between themselves and the individual children in the class or group.

The title of the book from which I am quoting, *Dyslexia or Illiteracy?*, shows that it is principally concerned with reading problems, hence with children of an age at which they would normally have been expected to be able to read. The principal remedy proposed is daily, individual help from parents, "paired reading," beginning with books so easy that the child can cope with them.

My purpose in writing this book, as it was with the earlier one, is not to propose solutions but to help parents and children avoid problems by doing enjoyable things together before the possible problems arise.

Not surprisingly, Young and Tyre, the authors of *Dyslexia or Illiteracy?* also decided to give advice to parents based on their professional experience. They wrote a guide for parents, *Teach Your Child to Read,* which was published in the same year (1985) and by the same publisher (Collins Fontana) as the paperback of my own *Anything School Can Do . . .* The chapters about choice of books, on "reading to learn," the observations on parents' relationship with children through reading I found admirable.

One mother said, "He was reading to me and it must have been the expression he put into it, but suddenly I realised until then I'd only thought of him as a baby, an *it*. For the first time I saw him as a person!" If parenting were simply a matter of feeding children, cleaning them and keeping them warm, there would be a lot more abandoned babies. Because parenting involves cultural transmission, we find them interesting and growing into people, and hang on to them! If, ultimately, they are going to manage without us and enjoy independence, then in a literate world we must make them highly literate.

An admirable book from which I shall quote again. Unfortunately it is also out of print. The advice on beginning reading was unlike mine in that it progressed from pictures to picture books to parents reading from picture books and helping children to "pick up" reading as they go along. However, the authors did say that not every child would follow the lines of development they had outlined; some might skip some stages, some stick at another and so on, that each child and parent will find their own route together. So I sent a copy of my own book to Peter Young, together with a copy of the dissertation on the subject that I had done for my linguistics diploma, and received in return a most encouraging letter, with this valuable sentence, "And, although we don't treat your E 3D C approach in our book we're in no doubt that, used in the way and at the time you advocate, it has everything to commend it—my own granddaughter is a living proof!"

I learn from the Open University publication that Peter Young has been a senior inspector of primary education and tutor at the Cambridge Institute of Education, that he was a member of the Warnock Committee, that he has written series of books for schools and is joint editor of the Open University series in which the book appeared.

Such well-informed support seemed to me to justify re-publication of the parts of my earlier book which focus on reading. Looking over the book again, I recognised that the account of how our children learnt could quite well be sifted out from recollections of painting and cooking and described more clearly. This is what I have tried to do in the first half of this book.

This second half, on the "Debate" is taken with a few additions from what I published in 1983. It is clear that my recommendations are tightly linked with getting in early but on the other hand matching sounds with letters and letter clusters; word-building, even sandpaper letters are the staple of centres which set out to remedy "dyslexia." Because the word "reading" is found in the title of this present book it is likely that parents of older children who have not learnt so easily may turn to it. I hope they find something useful—as I say, schemes to remedy dyslexia often use materials similar to those I describe. Indeed, the picture cards we made were based on an article in a now forgotten magazine, *Housewife,* about helping a child who had reading problems, but it must be clear from what I have written that the book I would recommend is *Dyslexia or Illiteracy?*

For my part, the reason I recommend early reading is not simply that we and our children enjoyed it; it is linked with Professor Jerome Bruner's commendation of "the style of care that increases the child's capacity to manage its own attention." This is close to Montessori's concern. The following paragraphs from *Children's Minds* by Margaret Donaldson, published in 1978 with the blessing of Professor Bruner, are relevant:

Piaget's findings and arguments are complex, but one point that emerges very clearly is that *awareness* typically develops when something gives us pause and when consequently, instead of just acting, we stop to consider the possibilities of acting which are before us. The claim is that we heighten our awareness of what is actual by considering what is possible. We are conscious of what we do to the extent that we are conscious also of what we do *not* do—of what we might have done. The notion of *choice* is thus central.

We cannot expect to find any simple answer to such a momentous question—but observe how, here again, learning to read may have a highly significant contribution to make . . . the lasting character of the print means that there is time to stop and think, so that a child has time to consider possibilities—a chance of a kind he may never have had before.

Thus it turns out that those very features of the written word which encourage awareness of language may also encourage awareness of one's own thinking and be relevant to the development of intellectual self-control, with incalculable consequences for the development of the kinds of thinking which are characteristic of logic, mathematics and the sciences.

Well, if learning to read may encourage awareness of one's own thinking and be relevant to the development of intellectual self-control, it seems reasonable to start earlier rather than later. However, even if an early start were accepted (and Donaldson does not decisively advocate this) there would remain several features of our preferred method which many teachers would find objectionable. In the following sections I intend to consider each of these elements separately, insofar as this is possible.

This preferred method is the *early* presentation of *three-dimensional capital letters*, identified *phonically* and encouraged *at home*.

In the introduction I explained briefly that over a period of years I was in a position to compare both short-term and long-term results of this method with the range of other accepted methods: sentence recognition, whole word recognition, phonic with lower-case letters, tracing and writing before reading. All the "subjects" were taught at home; all had the same teacher; all were quite well provided with nursery rhymes and word-games; all were read to for years and years.

Early Presentation

The first reason for encouraging an early start is enjoyment, both for children and parents. Building blocks, reading and painting give the best opportunities for visible achievement; sand and water give agreeable and useful experience but there is not much to show for it. At the age of two there is a great deal of satisfaction to be had from mastering a single letter, much more from a single written word. A single word has rich significance for a young child who is still making one or two words do the work of a sentence. Not so for a six-year-old for whom "flash cards" carry minimal meaning, while even the sentences used in school readers are lifeless. Asher Cashdan, an authority on reading, observes,

> Most British teachers expect their students to start the serious business of learning to read some time in their first or second school year, when the children are aged five or six.
>
> The carefully constructed reading primer is always an unsatisfactory compromise. Whether it depends on vocabulary control or on phonic restriction, the child is being asked to read

material he would never deliberately seek to listen to or say himself.

The Reading Teacher, January 1973.

In contrast I have a tape recording of Ivan, aged two and a half, puzzling out a set of picture cards (described in chapter four.) You can hear him: "C.CAR...CARROT!" And the shout, "I read it! I *read* it!"

Reading, however you define it, is a mysterious skill. It is most natural that children should acquire it at different rates. But the time available cannot be easily extended forwards from a late start; many authorities hold that children who are not reading easily at eight are not likely to become fluent readers. I suggest that an early start allows the symbols on which the whole structure is built to sink down into the depths of consciousness, so that it seems impossible to remember a time when S didn't identify itself as "ssss". The stages that follow, from sounding out SIT to allowing "sesquipedalian" to pour smoothly off the page into the mind will have room to build themselves up organically.

And even while teaching "phoneme-grapheme correspondence," that is, the sounds that match letters, we are incidentally pre-empting a different set of problems; we are using the word "letter",the word "sound," a little later the word "word," and doing so at the very time when children are most apt to absorb new words and meanings. Note that when we first ask about "letters" we are handling objects as easy to identify as buttons. Later we are talking about lines on paper which are recognisably pictures of those objects. When we begin to talk about "words" we are talking about a selection of these objects which together correspond to a single sound, and that sound to an idea, like ZOO. I had not myself realised how valuable that slow-motion introduction might be until I read the following passage from an article, "Linguistics for Infants" by Dr John Downing.

> A child can be quite normal in his own language development and that language can be the standard language of his reading books, and yet he is faced with many confusing words unknown in the reading instruction register. He may speak words, yet not know that he speaks "word" units. He may articulate perfectly, showing a clear distinction between phonemes such as /f/ and /k/, without knowing what he is doing or how he does it. But in developing literacy skills he has to become aware of his own language behaviour if he is to understand how written language operates.
>
> Consider the cognitive confusion aroused by a statement such as the following:
>
> "I'm going to boke some nittirs. See these nittirs. Their names are ooth and op. They say 'hgugh'. Who knows a dosp with the zoon 'hgugh' in it?"

I would not have risked using this example if I had thought of it myself. Dr Downing explains that "boke" = write; "nittirs" = letters; "ooth" = sea; "op" = aitch; "hgugh" = the final sound in Scottish "loch"; "dosp" = word; "zoon" = sound. Downing says that the confusion is much worse for the young child because he cannot translate these terms as an adult can. The child does not have the concepts. I think you will find that, even as an adult, it will take you a minute or so to work it out.

These are examples of the technical concepts of language that must be unknown at some time in every child's life and which he must eventually understand if he is to benefit from the teacher's instruction in reading. Most important of all, the pupil needs such concepts for his thinking about language and reading. Furthermore, these are only some of the simplest examples of the many phonological and syntactical concepts that need to be understood.

J Downing, "Linguistics for Infants," *Reading II*, 2,77.

A later paragraph in the same article indicates that such difficulties are widespread.

Turning to the more formal evidence for the importance of children's understanding of concepts of language, there is already extensive evidence for the truth that normal school beginners do not usually understand these technical linguistic concepts. Reid's Scottish five-year-olds had a great poverty of linguistic equipment to deal with the new experiences, calling letters "numbers" and words "names" and so on. Numerous studies by a variety of research methods have confirmed that the beginner's perception of *speech* segments does not coincide with the units *spoken word* and *phoneme* as conventionally represented in the written form of the language Chappell (1969); Downing (1970 and 1972); Downing and Oliver (1974); Evans (1974); Holden and MacGinitie (1972); Huttenlocher (1964); Karpova (1955).

There follows a similar set of citations showing that beginners have been found to be confused about the concepts relating to writing: *writing, written word, letter, number,* etc. I do not, by the way, intend to include all these references in the bibliography of this book, but it is worth mentioning that Karpova (1955) refers to an article in *Voprosy Psikhol. 4.*

The illuminating example of the "zoons of nittirs" illustrates some of the difficulty I have found in organising this section, "the debate about reading." It might be equally appropriate to the sub-section on "Identified phonically" but it seemed more useful to emphasise that teaching as early as possible that letters are "letters" is valuable in itself.

I hope you will keep it in mind while looking at another important argument in favour of early reading: it used to be normal, and that within living memory. Marjorie Fisher in *Intent Upon Reading*, a commentary upon children's books suited to various purposes, remarks that in the nineteen-twenties books were mostly bought for the children of reading families, who moved quickly from their primers to *The Wind in the Willows.* "Nowadays," she adds, "among the countless thousands of children demanding books for first solo reading, there are many who read late, at six or seven instead of at four or five."

A generation before, we find Compton Mackenzie annoyed about being interrupted when word-building with blocks before he was two, while Evelyn Waugh said in an interview, "My mother taught me the rudiments, and I think she taught them well."

Probably many mothers of Waugh's contemporaries did the same, but we do not happen to be told about them.

Slightly further back well-known names turn up; for example the Bronte sisters or William Morris, whose reading at four or five is mentioned in biographies, though not as anything remarkable; but I cannot resist a finer example, Thomas Arnold a child who, at the age of three, had been presented by his father, as a reward for proficiency in his studies, with the twenty-four volumes of Smollett's *History of England*.

John M Hughes in *Reading and Reading Failure* gives a convenient summary of some research in this field to which I have quite often seen reference:

Professor Durkin carried out an experiment at the University of Illinois which involved carefully controlled comparison of thirty children who had learned to read before six years with those who had learned to read later. By the end of the third year of schooling, the early readers were still one year ahead on average. Durkin found that all the parents of the early readers had noticed that their children had taken an interest in reading before the age of four. All these parents had assisted their children in identifying letters, numbers, words and sounds. But above all, they had spent time answering their questions and discussing the meanings of words. The parents of late readers generally accepted that reading should be taught by a teacher in school. These parents were also too busy to respond to the possibility that their children were ready to learn to read.

Margaret M Clark looked for early readers and wrote a book about them, *Young Fluent Readers*. She reported that they did not at all correspond to the stereotype of the rather feeble young scholar wearing glasses and unable to relate to his age-group. She found all her subjects lively, good mixers, interested, self-directed. Her conclusion was that any research on reading acquisition that did not take such children into account was inadequate.

I have implied that early learning takes place at home. In fairness, I should mention a couple of reports on planned classes in early reading: *L'Apprentissage précoce à la lecture* (Cohen 1978) where the class was in a bilingual school in Paris, and a paper by William Fowler in *Interchange* 2/2 (Ontario Institute of Education, 1971.) I know about the former because I met Dr Rachel Cohen during a conference of the International Reading Association that was held near Paris. We were brought to visit some classes, school and pre-school, to see how reading was taught. Rachel and I both thought that what we saw was unimaginative and inappropriate, but it seemed we were alone in believing that "earlier is easier."

Only at the end of the conference did we find quite unexpected support for our views from the president of the United Kingdom Reading Association. I shall mention him again.

Three – Dimensional

Just another way of saying "solid." Anything flat, on a smooth surface of paper or other material, is said to have two dimensions, length and width. Anything solid has three dimensions, length, width and depth or height or thickness. Common sense tells us that a baby is more likely to take notice of a solid object she can touch than of marks on paper. We have already seen that a fair amount of experience is needed before a baby can make any sense out of even a simple picture.

Russian studies have shown that children aged three who did not respond to squares and triangles shown on a screen learned to respond correctly after they had prolonged opportunity to handle solid squares and triangles. A paper by E Gibson (1970) gives further support to the common-sense assumption:

> Solid objects, which possess depth at their edges, are discriminated earlier than two-dimensional pictures or line drawings. If perceptual learning occurs in the earlier phase it involves a discovery of invariant properties of the object which the stimulation itself specifies

and which are critical for distinguishing one object from another. What is learned is learned in isolation from the background or differentiation rather than with an associative meaning for depth ... Ability to discriminate those features of objects which are critical for identification may transfer to outline drawings such as letters, but some critical features of letters remain to be discriminated after four years of age. The process again is one of differentiation rather than association. ("Development of perception: discrimination of depth compared with discrimination of graphic symbols." *Cognitive Development in Children,* Chicago, 1970)

Further, I urge the possibility that children who have the chance to learn early, using the sense of touch as well as sight, getting to know each letter familiarly, are less likely to emerge as dyslexic. The methods I propose are very like those used with children of six and seven who have been diagnosed as dyslexic. Below I quote part of a letter from Dr Graham Curtis Jennings, of Staines. I had seen him on television, explaining how he was able to identify children who were likely to be found, later, to be dyslexic. I wrote to him. He replied:

You have of course hit the nail on the head in your approach, namely, to use a multisensory approach coupled with early introduction of reading material graduated to developmental ability.

My problem in Ashford is that teachers are

(i) ignorant of the possibility that some children might have a genetically determined disorder that prevents the acquisition of the skills of reading and writing and (ii) that even if they believe it exists I couldn't as a doctor know anything about it.

So my job is to build bridges. I teach anyone who will listen to me; teachers, parents, doctors, nurses, health visitors. I write about it, lecture, even appear on TV!

Until the climate in the teaching profession is right I dare not let parents go to teachers with their anxieties. If they do, the teachers label them as worriers, trouble makers, etc. and become defensive and even label the child as coming from an anxious household!

It seems to me also that if the early multisensory approach is helpful to potential dyslexics, it is also true that a family that is geared to early learning for "ordinary" children is in a favourable position to give any handicapped child who may arrive a better start than they would otherwise have had.

Here you find me being inconsistent. I write of "potential dyslexics" though I have noted that Tyre and Young do not accept that word. The explanation is that letter and comment are taken from my own book, *Anything School Can Do....* which was published in the same year as *Dyslexia or Illiteracy?* so I had not had the opportunity to read it. It remains true that some children learn to read very easily indeed, others with relative difficulty. It must be an advantage to the latter to find themselves in a home where early, methodical reading instruction by a "multisensory approach" is a matter of course.

It happens that our second-last (tenth) child was late in learning to speak, We twice brought him to clinics to find out whether he was deaf or not and both times we were assured that he was not. He could hear a watch ticking. Later, when he was brought for an intelligence test he was given a high score. However, the psychologist remarked that he was reading very well for his age but that the errors he had made were of the kind they associated with partial deafness. Specialist advice was proposed, and it was found that his hearing was below average; it could be put right by the insertion of small plastic tubes; all would be well by the time he was twelve. It seems that his condition is not uncommon. If he had not been introduced to reading as early as possible, if we had left him to pick up what he could in school, he would probably have fallen quite far behind.

A "multisensory" approach might imply the association of sounds with colours or with music or movement. Dr Rachel Cohen, mentioned above, used something on those lines. My reliance was on solid objects which could be handled and put beside one another. Naturally, they were letters rather than words; a carved or moulded vocabulary would be limited.

Which letters, capital or lower-case, and why? These are questions which arouse surprisingly heated reactions. If you choose to take my advice and use capitals, you had better not mention the fact to anyone you do not know well until the child is quite advanced in reading.

IV

Capitals

Capital letters are still out of fashion. This is because "whole words" have for so long been seen as the normal starting point for learning to read. We shall return to the question of "whole words" and the reasons why they were adopted. For the moment, enough to say that this approach is based on the observation that different words have different shapes, that these shapes are what we take in when reading. The shapes depend on the projections of various letters above and below the line of print *in lower case*. Whole words in capitals do not look as different from one another as do the same words in lower case: compare CAPITAL and CAPTAIN with capital and captain. Those who advocate a whole word approach do not find capital letters acceptable; not only are primers all in lower-case, but in consequence so is the text in almost all picture books and in everything that is offered to children outside school. It is easy to buy plastic alphabets in lower case, while capitals are scarce. Oddly enough the long tradition of putting capital letters on building blocks continues, showing that the other is the innovation.

But *if* individual letters can be shown to be a good introduction to reading, then capitals have every advantage over lower case. They are the real letters, the forms into which the alphabet evolved over many centuries from the Phoenicians, through the Greeks, to the Roman perfection of Trajan's column. Evolution required that they develop in such a way as to be easily distinguished, one from the other.

Early Latin manuscripts were written in capitals (and without spaces between words!) Gradually, as scribes in a hurry rounded angles and joined letters together forms changed. By the fourth century AD our lower case had emerged, under pressure. Remember that everything there was to read had to be written, one off, by hand; not only no printing, but no typewriters, no photocopiers.

The standard capitals remained while different centres made different changes in writing styles. Charlemagne, around AD 800, employed the monk Alcuin to collect these varieties and design a uniform system. A beautiful job he did, and the first printed letters, six hundred years later, were based on these manuscript forms. By now printing has developed a great variety of typefaces, but all those that use what we still call the Roman alphabet follow a uniform code, with "f" rising above the line, "j" descending. Designers of typefaces aim to produce shapes which blend harmoniously with one another and which are legible *when assembled into words*.

The result is that lower case "c" and "e" are more alike than are "C" and "E"; m, n, h, r, resemble each other more closely than do M, N,

H, R. By far the most confusing are the four, b, d, q, p, which are the same shape but reversed or turned upside down.

Of course there are ways to tackle these difficulties. Those two of our children who were introduced to reading according to the instructions in the *Beacon Teacher's Manual* had trouble for a long time with "b" and "d". (Note to readers who are reading this section first: the *Beacon* series itself we found most useful, with traditional stories and smooth progression.) I pointed out to them that the word "bed" is rather the shape of a bed, and they could refer to this when confused. This still required them to find a remedy for confusion that the others never experienced.

What is more, the remedy depended on having a printed word in front of them and having grasped the left-to-right convention. If you offer a small child three-dimensional lower case letters you have to give, in effect, four different names to the same object, as if you were to say that something was a scissors when the point was towards you, a shears when pointing away, a cutter when facing right, a secateur when facing left.

Nobody denies that capital letters are easier to distinguish than lower case; the Bullock Report, *A Language for Life* says more or less what I have just said but uses a doll as example instead of the scissors. (Not such a convincing example, since there are treasured upsidedown dolls who have two heads and therefore two names.) Gibson, in the research quoted, says that difficulty with rotation may continue until age eight.

Just as capital letters are easier to identify, they are easier to write. Marion Richardson in *Writing and Writing Patterns*, which we found valuable, gives plenty of practice with capitals before moving on to continuous writing. (I hesitate to mention this series because for a long time after my previous book was published letters continued to arrive, asking for further details about where to get materials I had mentioned. I shall put all the information I have into the section on Resources)

Another advantage of beginning with capitals is that you can let the child use a typewriter; if you keep it in shift lock the letters that appear match those on the keyboard; when the time comes to add lower-case the typewriter or computer shows which form belongs to which capital letter.

Lastly, consider how often important, even vital, messages are delivered in capitals:

DANGER STOP KEEP OUT
POISON IN OUT PUSH PULL
POST OFFICE TOILETS BUS
LOOK LEFT LOOK RIGHT
CROSS NOW

When children are taught capitals they have nothing to unlearn. The initial teaching alphabet, (i.t.a.) is/was an interesting scheme which had quite a long spell of popularity; it may be still in use in some schools. One of the problems of reading the English language is that at least forty-four sounds have to be indicated by twenty-six letters. The i.t.a. scheme seeks to remedy this by providing forty-four symbols, some identical with ordinary letters, others modified, each representing one sound or phoneme. It was found that children using this began to read more easily but the difficulty remains that unless the whole community goes over to i.t.a.—which was never the aim of the designers—children must at some time make the transition to ordinary letters. As usual, some children, who were reading very well, made the transition with ease. (Who can be sure that they were not reading ordinary books at home?) Others fell back into confusion. The reasonable suggestion was made that no child should be asked to change until he or she was reading with ease. This might conflict with the need to move children up through higher classes.

Since i.t.a. appears to be fading out it might seem that there is no need for me to mention it. In fact years of research and substantial amounts of money for training, printing and so on were invested in it. Ladybird books were published in i.t.a. The assumption behind it is that whole words in lower case, or something closely resembling lower case, are the natural introduction to reading, but at the same time the invention itself acknowledges that learning in this way with the standard alphabet brings confusion.

I would submit that an early start with phonic capitals may be expected to get any child to the same point *at least* as a school-age start with i.t.a., while presenting them with nothing they need to un-learn.

V

Identified Phonically

By this I mean simply that if you accept the arguments for offering three-dimensional capital letters to young children, a sound rather than a name is the most economical and efficient way of identifying each one. There is no need for English letter-names until you want to spell, or to have someone spell, a word over the telephone—and believe me, if the person spelling something to you is not a native speaker of English this can be fairly bewildering. Just about everyone else in Europe calls A, "Ah", while the name we use of A, "Ay", commonly means E. "Ee", of course, signifies I!

On the telephone, even when we share the same convention for naming letters, we quite often have to resort to A for Arthur, C for Charlie and so on. Two people in the same room do not really need to spell a word aloud, they can write it and read it. The only circumstances I can think of in which letters are constantly referred to by name is in play, whether Scrabble or crosswords. Crosswords are, on the whole, a private pursuit. I can assure you that families that have been reared phonically play Scrabble and "I spy" in their own way with as much enjoyment as anyone else.

This may sound strange to parents. I have met people who were themselves at Montessori school, where they must have learnt the letters with the sounds of short vowels and hard consonants, as explained in Chapter Three, in the first part of this book, but who had completely forgotten that they had learnt sounds before meeting letter-names. So, if you feel that it is mere crankiness to call a letter by anything other than its name, I ask you to consider for a moment the steps that must be taken by a beginner who has been taught the names:

"Pee says 'puh,' eye says 'ih,' en says 'n,' so this word must be pin."

Go through the same steps with *India, wagon, octagon*, then try sounding the letters instead. The second "i" in India is a little different from the first, but neither is "eye." Some of us can remember the introduction of decimal coinage though we prefer to forget what could be bought then for a shilling, the present 5p. For quite a long time we had to mentally translate every 5p and 10p into shillings in our heads. (The shillings had twelve pence.) Letter names are similar obstacles to instant understanding.

Research results are clear. Dr John Downing (*Reading*, Vol 8, No 3) reports that three independent experimenters (Ohnmacht 1969; Johnson 1970; Samuels 1971) have all monitored the results of teaching letter names under rigorous scientific control and all reached the same conclusion—that letter name teaching gives the child no help whatsoever in learning to read.

On the other hand, it is allowed that children who know the names may learn sooner than children who do not; the probability is that they come from reading homes and see reading as an acceptable occupation.

This warning about letter-names is directed towards parents rather than teachers, who are unlikely to begin with anything other than words. I think we can reasonably suppose that practice in many schools would resemble that recommended in John M Hughes's excellent book, *Reading and Reading Failure*:

> When phonic teaching is based on a child's sight vocabulary and language experience, it means that he is taught to recognise whole words—for example, "dog"—before he is taught the sounds of the symbols "d", "o", "g". At the beginning stage of reading the word "dog" is more meaningful than the three symbols from which it is formed. The foundation of phonics is established once the child has acquired a number of sight words and the teacher brings the child's attention to the sounds associated with the initial letters of these known words.

This paragraph describes exactly the mistake which I believe is inherent in the most usual methods of teaching reading. I have mentioned in the introduction to this book that I used this approach, in different ways (Beacon and Doman) with four of our children and that later I found that it took them about two years longer to learn to read independently than the five children who were brought up on Early 3-D Phonic Capitals. Delay of this kind is not noticed in the school system where all are taught in the same way and there is no means of comparison. Most children learn to read in the end.

However, I do from time to time encounter long-term results that are not so satisfactory. I have remarked elsewhere that Esperanto is completely consistent; every word is pronounced as it is spelt, every letter retains the same sound. When I teach this language to adults I find that while most take advantage of this system others stumble over quite straightforward words in a way that shows that they have not the knack of scanning a word from left to right and producing a sound to match. I believe them to be victims of "whole word" instruction in childhood.

The problem has deep enough roots to require a section to itself.

VI

Letters or Words

Mr. Hughes's explanation of how to teach "d" brings us back full circle to the question of whether children should be introduced to letters before (written) words or (written) words before letters. His case rests on the assumption that the word "dog" is more meaningful than the three symbols of which it is formed. It all depends. For a household like ours, where "D" was familiar well before the age of two, and was known as "Dada's letter" while canines in general were still (rather alarming) bow-wows, and when we had one of our own she was known only as Sherry (she slept in a small sherry cask) the assumption is not valid.

(Incidentally, if we had used "d" it would have been not only dada's letter but also barbara's and pierce's and possibly also the queen's.)

The argument, as I have said, is circular. If you use phonic 3-D capitals, you can introduce them early. You can build up blending and reading very gradually, at an age when children feel that even single words are full of power. Once phonically regular words are being read with ease it is not difficult to introduce further letter clusters. Once the more frequent letter-clusters are known, the reader will be able to get the hang of enough of any suitable text to be able to make use of contextual clues to less regular words. By this stage she should be able to accept even the most difficult convention, the final "E" that usually signals that the previous vowel is long. Once this lesson has been absorbed, the child is practically independent.

While all this is going on, lower case letters can be linked with their capital sources, and all that remains is the search for something interesting to read.

If, on the other hand, you choose to teach (written) words before letters you lose the advantages both of capital letters and of a multisensory approach. (Complete carved words would be neither convenient nor useful.) True, you hope, as we all do, that children will have books and that books will be read to them, but that is a common factor whether words or letters are taught first. It may be the most important; no matter what introduction they are given, children who never meet an attractive book in loving surroundings are not likely to be lured into reading for themselves, but this does not alter the comparison between word first/letters first.

Those who favour words are likely to introduce them in either of two ways; gradually, with a "reading readiness programme" or directly and early. Glenn Doman, with his book *Teach Your Baby to Read*, made early recognition into a system. Children may spontaneously recognise very early a few significant words. Peter Ustinov's mother had an amusing story of Peter, as a babe in arms, rousing a whole busload of passengers with his excitement about the word OXO on an advertisement hoarding.

When you try to extend this sort of recognition you are likely to run into problems.

I used this system with our last two children because I had been impressed by Doman's arguments in favour of early reading. The elder of these two had a problem with hearing and this delayed speech. On the day that he first spoke, at the age of two years and three months, he "read" and remembered four words. Soon afterwards his fifteen-month-old brother began to recognise his favourite and unfavourite words, even selecting the card with the word BED and throwing it on the floor to show that he didn't want to go.

We had months of enjoyment, making jokes about snails and worms and members of the family, but by the time they had a "reading vocabulary" of about 120 words, confusion and frustration set in. New words too often had roughly the same appearance as words they knew, even though I had made some in capitals, some in lower case, to increase variety. When I tried to introduce letter sounds they were unwilling to backtrack and sound them out . They resented the fact that the magic was fading; they believed that the written word was something that should convey meaning at a glance. A well-intentioned short-cut had been misleading.

Our experience was close to that of mothers who replied to a survey reported by Asher Cashdan in *Where?*, the education magazine of the Consumers Association, in July 1968. Two-thirds of this sample enjoyed themselves; the children, average age two-and-a-quarter, learnt single words easily and rapidly, found the reading in the kit provided to be boring, and after a while became confused.

I am bound to add that, after a break, both of mine were reading quite competently at six and continued to be voracious readers but they were neither as competent nor as independent and not nearly as good at spelling as their five siblings who had made the smooth progression: letters, words, picture cards, then homemade books and a short run through a good reading series.

As for the more gradual introduction to which I referred, a "reading readiness programme" that consist of listening to sounds, looking at shapes, finding pictures that match, is commonly offered to children as a preparation for being taught to read by means of "sight-words" or "whole words." If you look at steps I suggest in Early 3-D you will see that similar exercises are included, but they are directly related to reading. The children match letters instead of matching spotted dogs. The dogs can be fun, but reading is more rewarding.

While writing this page have I come across this sentence from Andrei Sakharov's just published memoirs:

I began to teach myself to read at four, spelling out words on signboards and the names of steamships.

With those words Sakharov introduces a long list of books, Pushkin, Jules Verne, Hugo, Dickens, HG Wells, on to Goethe and Shakespeare and adds,

I remember discussing with Grandmother almost every page of Tolstoy's *Childhood, Boyhood, Youth* and *War and Peace*—a whole world of people "whom we know better than our own friends and neighbours." I entered adolescence enriched by these books and many others.

VII

The Background to "Whole Words"

Hornbooks and alphabet rhymes go back through centuries; parents tend to teach letters in spite of teachers' disapproval, so why such widespread insistence on "whole word" instruction throughout the English-speaking world?

We have seen that teaching letter names does not help children and that teaching both names and sounds too soon imposes an extra burden, but why does the educational establishment not encourage parents to use letter sounds?

This used to puzzle me until I came across *Reading and the Psychology of Perception*, by Hunter Diack (1963). He explained that the idea of introducing children to reading by means of whole words instead of letters grew up in the United States between 1820 and 1840. The trend was boosted by an investigation by J McK Cattell in 1885 which proved that adult readers could perceive only three or four *unrelated* letters during a brief exposure; if the letters were related, if they were words, the subjects could grasp up to twenty four letters during the same exposure. This delivered a damaging blow to the alphabetic method of teaching. Diack says:

Sixty years after Cattell's experiment some 10,000 books and articles about the teaching of reading could be found; in only a negligible number of them was it suggested that children should learn letters before words.

Indeed, in 1974 Professor Patrick Groff of San Diego University wrote in *Reading* (Vol 8, No 4) that "the invention called *sight words* was in as high esteem as ever." He proceeded to undermine the system by showing that out of a list of 238 high-frequency words only twenty per cent have a shape of their own, not duplicated by some other frequently used words, e.g. nest, rest; drink, drunk; frock, knock.

Hunter Diack found that words did not even have to resemble each other as closely as those examples to give rise to confusion. In a classroom full of children who had been taught whole words he wrote *aeroplane* on the blackboard; they all cheerfully shouted "elephant!" That large animal was the only long word on their flash cards.

In his book Diack mentioned that his own daughter had mastered most of the letters from Lexicon cards and had begun to read somewhere between two and three years of age. To support an article I was writing, I wrote and asked him why he had not continued to teach her to read. He replied that he did; that when she went to school at the usual age she was deliberately "untaught." His own word. Hunter Diack proceeded to write a phonically based reading scheme, *Royal Road*

Readers, which I have more than once seen commended.

If, then, the "sight word" theory has been shown to be mistaken, why does it persist? Partly, I suppose, because there is some truth in it. Nobody *who has learnt to read* spells out words, indeed, it seems that the upper half of a line of print provides all the clues we need. (Why, then, not teach children to recognise just the upper halves of words?) Then there is the defeatist belief that English spelling is so irrational that the only hope is to learn to recognise each word, as if it were Chinese.

Timing may have been relevant. Cattell's investigations were made at a time when teachers were coming to see themselves as professional persons. His findings were sanctified in training colleges, built into sets of readers. Discussion of teaching methods was probably based on those primers and extended through those 10,000 books and articles so that it came to be as much taken for granted as the movement of the sun around the earth in pre-Copernican Europe.

This is not mere speculation. I came across an article in *Reading* which showed how refusal to accept the "alphabetic method" can persist in spite of evidence. A group of English teachers visited schools in Finland. They found that teachers in Finland do not consider reading to be a problem. In the first eight weeks of school the class had read thirty-four pages of their reader (in capital letters) and had learnt the name and associated phonemes of thirteen letters of the twenty-one letter alphabet. The later stories in the same reader had quite complex plots and a wide vocabulary, yet the visitors' final comment was, "No one would advocate starting school at seven and *returning* (my italics) to the alphabetic method."

Even when "phonics" had been on the agenda for a good while in Britain (as in the books of John M. Hughes) they were still alien in Ireland. When giving talks to women's clubs I found that parents were being compelled to "hear" spellings—letter names—from their six year old children; one mother said her child had come to hate *her* because of this. Over a period I attended lectures and workshops at Teachers' Centres, where I met even remedial teachers who had never seen a phonic scheme set out; they were teaching remedial children with the very same whole-word and spelling methods that had already baffled the children. During the international reading congress in Paris which I have mentioned, Dr Cohen and myself, as well as a sympathetic Swiss teacher, noticed that there also remedial children were being taught by exactly the same method which had already baffled them. The only difference was that they were in smaller groups, were rather older, and were manifestly bored.

It is ironic that they were being taught by a syllabic method—for them "whole words" would at least have made a change.

I am sure remedial teachers have by now caught up on phonics, but the readers my grandchildren have to use in school are as dreary as those my own children almost escaped. Perhaps I should explain that "almost." One of the boys was unlucky enough to find himself in First

Class at a boys' school; they were being asked to
read some rubbish about a mouse *backwards* from
the bottom of the page, in case they knew the
page by heart and deceptively appeared to be able
to read it. We sent him at that age because we
were warned that if we delayed we would not be
able to get him in at all. A long delay would have
been so much better for him. Most of the rest of
the family started school at an age when their
classmates might be expected to be able to read.

VIII

Encountered at Home

I have already argued in favour of home as the place for early learning and for early learning as a way to make life at home more enjoyable for both generations—even for three. The nineteen-month-old grandson whom I mentioned in the introduction runs to fetch his favourite book of nursery rhymes from his special corner as soon as he arrives here and carries it to me to read. I find that by now I am able to read it without my spectacles.

It must be obvious that the steps or stages I have been writing about—insets, letters, cards, books, "listen to me reading"—are activities which, if they are to happen at the age proposed, are very much more easily managed where there is only one child at that stage. It is quite helpful for the baby to have seen an older sibling manipulating insets, making them, as it were, socially acceptable. I shouldn't care to be trying to explain the process to two fifteen-month-olds at the same time. Concentration on letters and cards requires peace and quiet. Good Montessori schools provide peace for individual work but whenever I see groups of toddlers on TV there are always some of them shunting around on wheeled toys. Solitary workers may be protected, but only by the greatest vigilance. A nursery-school teacher wrote to *The Times Educational Supplement,* noting that while her training told her that young children's attention span was about five minutes, and while this matched her experience in the nursery school, she had recently realised that her little boy was able to concentrate for twenty or twenty-five minutes when he was at home.

Reading specialists are now saying that it would be a good thing if first reading could be taught on an individual basis. They sometimes suggest that senior pupils should be brought into the classroom to "hear" the younger children reading, or that retired people with time to spare might do the same. From time to time new "experiments" discover that children's reading improves if parents "hear" them at home; teachers send home a notebook in which the parents note that the recommended reading has been done.

At home reading can be locked into real life; at home there is no need to consult a record chart to find out just what each child is reading and what her problems may be; at home it is almost always possible to drop everything when a new reader demands a hearing.

Most important of all, to my mind, is the fact that while a teacher who has taught fifty or five hundred children to read will be pleased when number five-hundred-and-one cops on, she cannot be as delighted as a parent; number five-hundred-and-one will be pleased to be praised, but hardly as happy as when someone she loves enjoys her achievement along with her.

When I attended that first European Conference of the International Reading Association, I picked up a good deal of interesting information. In regard to learning at home, I noted that nearly eight per cent of children in Finland may be expected to be reading fluently when they start school at seven, while another twenty-eight per cent will have made a good start. In Madrid one quarter are usually fluent, another quarter familiar with the elements. Italian children start school at six; about thirty per cent are familiar with the elements. They are taught by means of capital letters associated with pictures and are expected to have mastered the structure of the word within three months and to be ready to move on to cursive writing.

We visited an *école maternelle* and also ordinary and remedial classes in primary school. In the *école maternelle* the syllables, ma, me, mu, etc. were written large, in cursive writing in blue-black ink on sheets from exercise books, pinned up high on a wall, and the children were expected to point with a long bamboo rod to the syllables making up the desired word; *rateau* was one I remember. The remedial class were, as I remarked above, being taught by the very same syllabic method that had already defeated them as if no one could think of any other way to teach. How could I refrain from thinking to myself, "Anything school can do, you can do better."

I found support for my own views both from this experience and from hearing about Finland (as I have noted before.) Even more supportive was an observation by Professor JE Merritt,

Professor of Educational Studies at the Open University. He remarked in passing, *"Any intelligent mother can teach her child to read better than any teacher."*

At the beginning of this part of the book, "The Debate about Reading," I commended two books by Peter Young and Colin Tyre, one published by the Open University, the other unfortunately already out of print. Two paragraphs from the latter ought to be put into circulation again:

Parents are Born Teachers.
Sexual reproduction in *homo sapiens* is far more subtle and complex than the elementary gymnastics of the sex manuals. The successful selection and courtship of mates is designed to provide mothers with protection during the vulnerable days of pregnancy and deliver., and for the survival and upbringing of the offspring during infancy.

The procreative drive is no more satisfied by the birth of the child than it was by orgasm. Survival of the species demands that the drive is only satisfied when the child attains physical, social, and intellectual maturity and independence. Babies have been given a two-shot genetic endowment from the species gene-pool which ensures that they are each unique. To realise their uniqueness and their full potential, they must be taught by their parents. Babies are born learners, programmed to survive by observing, exploring and thinking. They form hunches or hypotheses based on their perceptions of their surroundings, and they test them out. Having taught us to attach ourselves to them, they are quick to establish an interactive relationship. They want to learn. We want to teach them. We must catch the moment.

The baby-parent system is not a closed, but an open one. The basic survival programme is developed and orchestrated to equip the child with the traditions and behaviours appropriate to its community, society and culture. Nowhere is this more in evidence than in the way in which children learn and parents teach language. This is where parents excel. Because learning to read is part of learning language, we need to look at what parents do to teach language in greater detail. As Julian Huxley put it, "Man adds tradition to heredity."

Peter Young and Colin Tyre, *Teach Your Child To Read*, 1985.

I wish I had that passage at my disposal when I was writing about parent-directed reading acquisition as part of the graduate diploma in theoretical linguistics to which I have alluded in the Introduction.

Language acquisition was naturally part of that course. The data showed that clear naming of objects is not a special technique; it's what mothers everywhere do without instruction. The following paragraph is taken from JB Gleason, in *Talking to Children*, 1977.

We recognise now that language acquisition is an interactive process that requires not only a child with the appropriate neurological equipment in a state of readiness, but also an older person who engages in communicative interchange with him and with some objects out there in the world as well.

Parental labelling is an example of this: when looking at filmed or videotaped records one common thing is seen: the parent engages in some sort of naming behaviour while at the same time pointing at the object being named.

Another contribution to the same collection (Newport and Gleitman) says much the same thing at greater length; they say,

> In its strongest form, this claim is that the child can construct language only from a very carefully circumscribed kind of data, presented to the child selectively in correspondence with language growth,

and that the prime candidate for this task is the mother. More supportive still to my encouragement of saying "square, square" and "circle, circle" they continue;

> The basic position for which we will now argue is that the child is biased to listen selectively to utterance-initial items and to items presented in referentially obvious situations.

Exactly what I said myself.

Moving on to the details of reading instruction, my most useful source at that time was a two-volume collection, found in the library of the Irish Association for Applied Linguistics, *Theory and Practice of Early Reading*, ed. Resnick & Weaver, published in 1979 in the USA. This included substantial articles on a complete spectrum of views, from Goodman insisting that "learning to read is natural" and that children did not need to be taught, to Bateman, saying that the only certain cause of reading failure was the absence of incidental or systematic instruction:

the etiological classifications most useful to the educator are those that specify precisely what the child most needs to be taught about reading, for example, short vowel sounds, left-to-right decoding or sound blending.

Bateman discounted objections which were based on the fact that some children respond to *b* by saying *d* about half the time.

E Gibson, whose investigations into perception in depth I have already quoted, suggested that too heavy dependence on quantification may blind us to the great value of the clinical analysis of a few cases.

... in our current state of development a careful application of selected aspects of that knowledge to individual cases of developing readers and to the context in which their reading develops and their reading instruction occurs may produce promising hypotheses which can then be subjected to validation.

Which, I submit, fits my contribution, unplanned research into four approaches with eleven matched children, neatly enough.

Another article mentioned a report from Israel,

where, in the 1950s, standard practice was to introduce reading through phrase units; teaching of letter-sounds was not acceptable. Large scale immigration resulted in fifty per cent reading failure at the end of the first school year. Investigation showed that some classrooms were entirely successful, while some classrooms failed completely. The successful ones had independent-minded teachers who devoted a great deal of time to phonic drill and to breaking words into smaller units. It was also found that parents who were doing much the same thing had been "very helpful in overcoming the harmful effects of the holistic teaching practices of the day."

You see that word "parents"?

Well, since it is there I cannot say that it never appeared in the two volumes of Resnick & Weaver, but parents are not sufficiently significant to appear in the index. As you may suppose, they were the first people I looked for.

But publication in a book imposes delay. It is several years since I collected those references. There was a possibility that authorities on the teaching of reading might in the meantime have come to appreciate the advantages of early, home-based learning. When I had finished the rest of this present book I went to the ITE library and looked rapidly through the recent numbers of journals—*The Reading Teacher*, and the review of the International Reading Association. They were filled with statistical tables; one article had researched the interesting question of whether teachers who had MAs won more awards for teaching reading than teachers who were not so highly qualified; it seemed not. The overall impression: they are by teachers, or former teachers, about teachers, for teachers. The notion that teachers should preferably not be the people to help children during reading acquisition would undermine the whole construction.

That is why there is no place for such proposals as those of Peter Young and Colin Tyre. True, they have both been classroom teachers for many years; they worked together as joint consultants to the project for the teaching of reading for the National Development Programme for Computer Assisted Learning (which makes their insistence on parent-assisted learning all the more impressive.) One is a senior educational psychologist, the other has been a senior inspector of primary education and tutor at the Cambridge Institute of Education, member of the Warnock Committee, etc. My question is, does the average primary teacher know how much authoritative support there is for leaving initial responsibility to parents?

I would like to conclude this debate with a passage from a book, *The School in Question*, by Thorsten Husen, professor of education in the University of Stockholm, responsible also for research into education in many other countries besides his own:

> In Sweden . . .the church law of 1686 had made reading competence mandatory for marriage and participation in church ceremonies, such as the Last Supper. The parish priest examined all adults regularly, usually once a year, with regard to literacy and mastery of the scripture . . .

The literacy campaign was launched almost entirely without resort to formal schooling. In the last analysis the parents had the responsibility of seeing that the children learned to read, and the parents were controlled by the clergy. The overwhelming majority had achieved literacy in reading long before elementary schooling was made compulsory by legislation. Still, some 25-30 years later about one-fifth to one-third of all children were taught at home, and children who entered elementary school were expected to have acquired some basic reading skills at home ...

Almost universal competence in reading can be achieved, given adequate motivation, in a pre-industrial society without formal schooling.

Thorsten Husen, *The School in Question.*

RESOURCES

Phonically planned reading series:

I am very happy to be able to report that both the *Beacon Readers* and the *Fuzzbuzz* series which I have recommended are in print. Irish readers can order them through Books Upstairs, 36, College Green, Dublin 2. (Telephone: 01-679 6687.)

In both cases it is necessary to order the complete set. I have ordered the *Beacon Readers* and find that they will cost between £20 and £25. I would further recommend that if you choose the more modern *Fuzzbuzz* series you include the *Teacher's Manual*, which explains very helpfully the system on which the series is designed. Anyone who has read my account of teaching my own family will understand that I do not recommend the *Beacon Manual*.

Books Upstairs are ready to order, by computer, any book that is in print; they will, of course, tell you whether the book you are looking for is in print or not. Most other bookshops will provide the same service.

Geometric Insets and Letters.

The set of plastic insets which I have described can be had from Evans, school suppliers, Mary's Abbey,

Dublin 1. They also have a good, inexpensive set of capital letters in plastic. Well worth a visit to look at paints, coloured papers, etc.

Plastic capital letters with magnetic backing—a generous set with three examples each of A,E,I,O and U—are available in Early Learning Centres (Henry St. Dublin 1 and in other cities.)

They also have Form-boards and simple jigsaws.

As for home-made geometrical insets, I reproduce the information I gave in *Anything School Can Do, You Can Do Better* but it seems that, just as the human-powered lawn mower has been superseded by the electric model, it has become more and more difficult to buy the old-fashioned manual fret-saw.

You need a sheet of plywood, thick enough not to curl up, measuring about 36" by 18". This can be divided into 18 squares, more than you need, but leaving leeway for mistakes. On these squares draw the shapes as illustrated. To cut them out you need a fretsaw with spare blades, a support, a G-clamp to hold the support on a table, a fine drill to make the first hole. A hobbies or woodwork supplier should be able to supply these, and show you how to use them, or perhaps give you the name of someone with a power jig-saw who would make them for you. Once they are made and sandpapered, glue a suitable handle to the centre of each inset and paint inset and frame with polyurethane varnish or gloss paint.

I wish you luck with the hunt for the fretsaw. When I was eleven I made a wall bracket with curly edges and curved designs excised from the supports. Fretwork was so popular with my age group that children's magazines included patterns for such things. I got much satisfaction from making it. By the time I was in my twenties this fashion had faded but it was still possible to buy spare fret-saw blades in the village hardware shop. When she was eleven, out sculptor daughter used the fretsaw to make charming traditional children's toys. Now we have two neighbourhood delicatessens but no hardware shop, much less fretsaws.

Playdough

Many years ago I found a recipe. The quantities were, roughly, three cups of plain flour, a half cup of salt, a half cup of cooking oil. Mix, add water to make softish dough; knead until springy, keep in a plastic bag in refrigerator.

Small amounts of cooking colour or powder paint may be mixed in. The oil makes the dough pliable, the salt prevents mould. For play, the dough can be used over and over again for a long time. If objects made from it are baked in a slow oven they last even longer. The baby in our Christmas crib rests on a wreath of leaves and flowers that must be at least twenty-five years old.

Poems from the Beginning

BOW-BOW, SAYS THE DOG,
MEW, MEW, SAYS THE CAT,
GRUNT, GRUNT, GOES THE PIG,
AND SQUEAK, GOES THE RAT.

TOO, WHOO, SAYS THE OWL,
CAW, CAW, SAYS THE CROW,
QUACK, QUACK, SAYS THE DUCK.
AND WHAT CUCKOO SAYS, YOU
  KNOW.

****

HOW MANY MILES TO BABYLON?
THREE SCORE AND TEN.
SHALL I BE THERE BY
  CANDLELIGHT?
YES, AND BACK AGAIN.

****

LADIES GO NYM, NYM, NYM,
GENTLEMEN GO TROT, TROT, TROT;
OLD JACK GOES GALLOPPY,
  GALLOPPY, GALLOPPY
AND DOWN INTO A DITCH.

HIGGLEY PIGGELY, MY BLACK HEN,
SHE LAYS EGGS FOR GENTLEMEN.
SOMETIMES NINE AND SOMETIMES
  TEN,
HIGGLEY, PIGGLEY, MY BLACK HEN.

****

ONE, TWO,
BUCKLE MY SHOE.
THREE, FOUR, KNOCK AT THE DOOR.
FIVE, SIX,
PICK UP STICKS.
SEVEN, EIGHT,
LAY THEM STRAIGHT.
NINE, TEN,
A BIG FAT HEN.

****

LITTLE BOY BLUE
COME BLOW YOUR HORN,
THE SHEEP'S IN THE MEADOW,
THE COW'S IN THE CORN.
WHERE IS THE BOY THAT LOOKS
  AFTER THE SHEEP?
HE'S UNDER THE HAYCOCK, FAST
  ASLEEP.
SAY, WILL YOU WAKE HIM?
NO, NOT I,
FOR IF I DO HE'S SURE TO CRY.

THE BELLS OF LONDON

GAY GO UP AND GAY GO DOWN,
TO RING THE BELLS OF LONDON
  TOWN.
HALFPENCE AND FARTHINGS,
SAY THE BELLS OF ST MARTIN'S.
ORANGES AND LEMONS,
SAY THE BELLS OF ST CLEMENT'S.
PANCAKES AND FRITTERS,
SAY THE BELLS OF ST PETER'S.
TWO STICKS AND AN APPLE,
SAY THE BELLS OF WHITECHAPEL.

KETTLES AND PANS,
SAY THE BELLS OF ST ANN'S.
YOU OWE ME TEN SHILLINGS,
SAY THE BELLS OF ST HELEN'S.
WHEN WILL YOU PAY ME?
SAY THE BELLS OF OLD BAILEY.
WHEN I GROW RICH,
SAY THE BELLS OF SHOREDITCH.
PRAY WHEN WILL THAT BE?
SAY THE BELLS OF STEPNEY.
I AM SURE I DON'T KNOW,
SAYS THE GREAT BELL OF BOW.

HERE COMES A CANDLE TO LIGHT
  YOU TO BED,
HERE COMES A CHOPPER TO CHOP
  OFF YOUR HEAD.

                        ANON

LADYBIRD, LADYBIRD,
FLY AWAY HOME.
YOUR HOUSE IS ON FIRE
AND YOUR CHILDREN ALL GONE;
ALL EXCEPT ONE AND HER NAME IS
  ANN
AND SHE HID UNDER THE FRYING
  PAN.

****

SIMPLE SIMON

SIMPLE SIMON MET A PIEMAN
GOING TO THE FAIR;
SAID SIMPLE SIMON TO THE PIEMAN,
"LET ME TASTE YOUR WARE."

SAYS THE PIEMAN UNTO SIMON,
"SHOW ME FIRST YOUR PENNY";
SAYS SIMPLE SIMON TO THE PIEMAN,
"INDEED I HAVE NOT ANY."

SIMPLE SIMON WENT A-FISHING
FOR TO CATCH A WHALE;
ALL THE WATER HE HAD GOT
WAS IN HIS MOTHER'S PAIL.

SIMPLE SIMON WENT TO LOOK
IF PLUMS GREW ON A THISTLE;
HE PRICKED HIS FINGERS VERY MUCH
WHICH MADE POOR SIMON WHISTLE.

                                    ANON

BRIAN O'LINN

BRIAN O'LINN WAS A GENTLEMAN
  BORN,
HIS HAIR IT WAS LONG AND HIS
  BEARD UNSHORN.
HIS TEETH WERE OUT AND HIS EYES
  FAR IN—
"I'M A WONDERFUL BEAUTY," SAYS
  BRIAN O'LINN!

BRIAN O'LINN WAS HARD UP FOR A
  COAT,
HE BORROWED THE SKIN OF A
  NEIGHBOURING GOAT,
HE BUCKLED THE HORNS RIGHT
  UNDER HIS CHIN—
"THEY'LL ANSWER FOR PISTOLS." SAYS
  BRIAN O'LINN!

BRIAN O'LINN HAD NO BREECHES TO
  WEAR,
HE GOT HIM A SHEEPSKIN TO MAKE
  HIM A PAIR,
WITH THE FLESHY SIDE OUT AND
  THE WOOLLY SIDE IN—
"THEY ARE PLEASANT AND COOL,"
  SAYS BRIAN O'LINN!

BRIAN O'LINN HAD NO HAT TO HIS
  HEAD,
HE STUCK ON A POT THAT WAS
  UNDER THE SHED,
HE MURDERED A COD FOR THE SAKE
  OF HIS FIN—
"'T WILL PASS FOR A FEATHER," SAYS
  BRIAN O'LINN!

THE FAIRIES

UP THE AIRY MOUNTAIN,
DOWN THE RUSHY GLEN,
WE DAREN'T GO A-HUNTING,
FOR FEAR OF LITTLE MEN;
WEE FOLK, GOOD FOLK.
TROOPING ALL TOGETHER;
GREEN JACKET, RED CAP,
AND WHITE OWL'S FEATHER!

WILLIAM ALLINGHAM

Bibliography

Bateman, B. "Teaching Reading to Learning-Disabled Children and Other Hard-to-Teach Children," in Resnick and Weaver, pp. 227-252.

Beacon Readers. London: Ginn and Co, 1922.

Berger, P. *The Social Construction of Reality*. Harmondsworth: Penguin, 1977.

Bronfenbrenner, U. "A Report on Longitudinal Evaluations of Pre-School Programmes." Washington: 1974.

Bruner, J. *Towards a Theory of Instruction*. Harvard, 1975.

—*The Relevance of Education*. Harmondsworth: Penguin, 1974.

Bullock, A. *A Language for Life*. HMSO: 1975.

Cashdan, A. "Reflections on the Beginning Reading Program," *The Reading Teacher*, Vol. 26, No 4.

Chall, J.S. "The Great Debate; Ten Years Later," in Resnick and Weaver, pp. 30-34.

Clark, M.M. *Young Fluent Readers, What Can They Teach Us*? London: Heinemann, 1976.

Cohen, Dr R. *L'apprentissage précoce à la lecture*. Presses Universitaires de Paris, 1978.

Dally, A. *Inventing Motherhood*. London: Burnet Books, 1982.

Deakin, M. *The Children on the Hill*. London: André Deutsch, 1974.
(An outside observer's view of intensive home learning; rather intimidating)

Diack, H. *Reading and the Psychology of Perception*. Nottingham, 1963.
(Also Daniels and Diack, *Royal Road Readers*, a phonic series often commended.)

Donaldson, M. *Children's Minds*. London: Fontana, 1978.
(If you speak to children in their own language, you

147

may find that they understand more than Piaget recognised.)

Douglas, J.W.B. *The Home and the School, a Study of Ability and Attainment in the Primary School.* London: McGibbon & Kee, 1964.

Downing, J. "Some Curious Paradoxes in Reading Research," *Reading,* Vol 8, No 3, 2-10.

Edwards, B. *Drawing on the Right Side of the Brain.* London: Fontana, 1982.
(It seems likely that the importance of this book will be increasingly recognised; it is about much more than simply drawing. Strongly recommended.)

Eibl-Eibesfeldt, I. *Love and Hate.* London: Methuen, 1971.

Fisher, M. *Intent upon Reading.* London, 1961.

Fowler, W. "A Developmental Learning Strategy for Early Reading in a Laboratory Nursery School," *Interchange* 2/2. Ontario: The Ontario Institute for Studies in Education, 1971.

Frankenberg, S. *Commonsense in the Nursery.* London, 1922. (Reprinted Penguin.)

—*Latin with Laughter.* London, ?1930

Gibson, E. "Development of Perception: Discrimination of Depth Compared with Discrimination of Graphic Symbols," *Cognitive Development in Chidhood.* Chicago, 1970.

Glass, G.V. and Smith, M.L. "Meta-Analysis of Research on the Relationship of Class-Size and Achievement (1978)" and "Relationship of Class-size to Classroom Processes, Teacher Satisfaction and Pupil Effect: a Meta-Analysis (1979)." Far West Laboratory, 1855 Folsom Street, San Francisco, CA.

Gleason, J.B. "Talking to Children; Some Notes on Feedback," in Snow and Ferguson pp. 199-219.

Henderson, H. *The Politics of the Solar Age.* New York: Anchor Press, Doubleday, 1981.
(The success of GNP-measured economics rests on calling all home-based and maintenance activities

"non-productive." This fine book helps us to see how we support society by standing on our own two feet. It ranges very widely.)

Holt, J., ed. *Growing Without Schooling*. Boston

Hughes, J. *Phonics and the Teaching of Reading*. London: Evans Bros, 1972.

—*Reading and Reading Failure*. London: Evans Bros, 1975.

Hunt, J. McVicar. *Intelligence and Experience*. New York, 1961.

—*The Challenge of Incompetence and Poverty*. Illinois, 1969.

—"Social Aspects of Intelligence: Evidence and Issues," 1971.

—"Sequential Order and Plasticity in Early Psychological Development." (Paper presented to the Jean Piaget Society, Philadelphia, 1972.)

Illich, I. *Deschooling Society*. London: Calder & Boyars, 1971.

Leach, P. *Who Cares?* Harmondsworth: Penguin, 1971.

Lewin, R., ed. *Child Alive*. London: Temple Smith, 1975.

Lister, I. *Deschooling, A Reader*. Cambridge: Cambridge University Press, 1974.

(A collection of articles and extracts from sources on three continents which illustrate the fact that "more and more people are beginning to notice that majorities fail to learn what schools pretend to teach.")

Marshall, S. *An Experiment in Education*. Cambridge: Cambridge University Press, 1963.

McMahon, S. *The Poolbeg Book of Children's Verse*. Dublin: Poolbeg, 1987.

Montessori, M. *The Montessori Method. Scientific Pedagogy as Applied to Child Education in the "Children's Houses" with Additions and Revisions*. With introduction by J. McVicar Hunt. New York: Schocken Books, 1964.

Moore, R.S. & D.N. *Better Late Than Early. A New*

Approach to Your Child's Education. New York: Reader's Digest Press, 1977.

(Two highly qualified researchers show that there is no evidence to favour early schooling, much against. Adds constructive suggestions.)

Mullarney, M. *Anything School Can Do, You Can Do Better.* Dublin: Arlen House, 1983.

—*Esperanto for Hope.* Dublin: Poolbeg, 1989.

Newport, E.L., Gleitman, H. and Gleitman, L.R. "Mother I'd Rather Do It Myself: Some Effects and Non-Effects of Maternal Speech Style," in Snow and Ferguson, pp. 109-151.

Pines, M. *The Revolution in Learning.* London: Allen Lane, 1971.

(Investigation of several different approaches to early cognitive learning in the USA. Author notes that all roads seem to lead towards early reading.]

Polk-Lillard, P. *Montessori in Modern Approach.* New York: Shocken Books, 1975.

(Shows Montessori to be far ahead of her time in terms of psychology of learning.)

Popper, K. *Unended Quest: An Intellectual Auto-biography.* London: Fontana, 1976.

Porcher, M.A. and Winn, Marie. *The Playgroup Book.* New York and London: Souvenir, 1967.

Raven, J. *Education, Values and Society.* London, 1977

—*Parents, Teachers and Children.* Scottish Council for Research in Education, 1980.

(The first of Raven's books reports substantial research, much of which supports the view that our educational efforts are counter-productive. The second book is perhaps for specialists but includes this encouraging sentence: "From the data we have presented it seems likely that parents desperately want to enjoy their relationship with their children.")

Ravielli, A. *Wonders of the Human Body.* London: Harrap, 1955.

Remick, H. "Maternal Speech to Children During

Language Acquisition," in Von Raffler-Engel and Lebrun eds. *Baby Talk and Infant Speech*. Amsterdam: Swets and Zeitlinger B.V., pp. 223-234.

Resnick, B. and Weaver, P.A. *Theory and Practice of Early Reading*. New Jersey: Erlbaum, 1979.

Richardson, M. *Writing and Writing Patterns*. London, 1979.

Ridout, R. English Workbooks.

Snow and Ferguson eds. *Talking to Children*. Cambridge: Cambridge University Press, 1977.

Suzuki, S. *Ability and Development from Age Zero*. Ohio, 1981.

—*Nurtured by Love*. London, 1970.

Tizard, B. and Hughes, M. *Young Children Learning, Talking and Thinking, at Home and School*. London: Fontana, 1984.

Vygotsky, L.S. *Thought and Language*. MIT Press, 1927.

Waddell, H. *Stories from Holy Writ*. London: Constable, 1949.

Wells, J.C. *Jen Nia Mondo*. Middlesex, 1974 and Rotterdam, 1978.
(A series of introductory lessons in Esperanto—the living language which aims to solve the world's language problems by becoming a second language, neutral and simple, for all mankind.)

White, B.L. *Final Report, Child Rearing Practices and the Development of Competence*. Harvard, 1972.

Young, P. and Tyre, C. *Dylsexia or Illiteracy?* Open University Press, 1983.

—*Teach Your Child to Read*. London: Fontana, 1985.

Esperanto for Hope

A New Way of Learning
the Language of Peace

Máire Mullarney

POOLBEG